A STORY ABOUT FRIENDSHIP

How Disability changed my Life

Jamie,
Congrats on the
wedding coming up!
Meg
Dan Don

DANIEL ROSSI

Thanks be to God for the situations and experiences He has placed in my life...and of course Mom for your continual support, love, back-scratches, phone calls, enthusiasm, generosity, your tiramisu, taking care of my cat, the dance lessons during high school, teaching me how to drive, your tiramisu and your belief in leading through serving!

ACKNOWLEDGEMENTS

No book such as this one is the work of one person. A lifetime of friendships and relationships is what an author tries to pull together an articulation of what he or she has learned and hopes that others will find worth reading. I would like to thank Luanne Donahoe for her work on editing this book and her honesty throughout. I would also like to thank Jenny O'Brien who was greatly supportive of the idea and allowed me to share about the life of her son. I am deeply grateful for those that read the book in its rough draft and believed that it should be brought to this stage.

This book is dedicated to Greg O'Brien.
Thank you for teaching me about friendship!

CONTENTS

BY JENNY O'BRIEN

The birth of a baby is a joyful, exciting, life-changing event. As the perfect (well at least in our eyes) young family, we waited with great expectation, the birth of our second child. Our darling little girl Ashley, awaited the arrival of her first brother or sister. A proud dad and mom, looked forward to the millionaire family. Life was good.

It came as a bit of a surprise on Sunday morning back in September '86, a month before baby #2's scheduled arrival that I went into early labour. We headed to the hospital after dropping wee Ashley off at her favorite sitter, with promises she would soon have her very own live cabbage patch baby.

The rest, as they say, is history. After a relatively short 8 hours of labour the newest O'Brien entered this world. A boy!! 6 lbs, 1 ounce. We were delighted.

And then we heard the nurses say they needed a pediatrician – he was scoring low on the AGPAR – the test they did right after babies are born. Within an hour the doctors told us it appeared our little fellow had Down Syndrome – a condition of cognitive delay and possible physical concerns that they would verify with genetic testing. Suddenly, that perfect family, that good life, that much anticipated special delivery, was clouded by imperfection.

That's not to say we didn't love our beautiful new baby boy – Gregory. We did! But it was a scary new reality, dealing with an outcome no parents plan for or expect. The fears of 'what if' quickly dominated our thoughts. How will we manage? How will our lives change? How will we ever protect this vulnerable little baby against the big bad world? This wasn't the life we thought we would live. Nothing would be the same, or as good. Little did we know!

Fast forward 15 years. That 'perfect' life had taken a little detour from what we once envisioned, but we were happy. We'd learned to deal with the challenges of today and not worry too much about the challenges of tomorrow. We've seen our fair share of trials and tribulations. We've had therapies and interventions since the time Gregory was 5 weeks old. We've tried to leverage all the resources in the system and provide him with a normal and happy life. His integration into the school system was a generally positive experience – not perfect, but certainly better than we ever expected. Caring educators and support staff ensured his inclusion in the regular curriculum, adapting for him along the way. His social circle was limited but he was always the first person people acknowledged when we were at the mall or arena or walking the streets of Markham. He was a likeable little boy, but a boy who struggled to establish true friendships. Invited to the odd birthday party or maybe an afternoon at a friend's house, none of these relationships ever took root.

We did our best to ensure Greg had the experiences of any little boy. He was enrolled in swimming and soccer, t-ball and day camp. We were blessed that his limitations were mild compared to many of those similarly challenged. He could talk and make himself understood. He could participate in physical activities. He had a heart of gold and has always shown a high degree of sensitivity to others.

And then one summer day, we met Daniel. A chance meeting at a local pool, Greg's life would never be the same. From that first day, Dan interacted with Greg like any friend would, buddy to buddy. They splashed and carried on, as only two teenage boys can. My little guy - now not so little, but always my baby - was absolutely thrilled to have met a new friend. (To Greg, everyone was his friend). Mom was a little less convinced about this new friendship, having spent years trying to protect him from disappointment.

Well my fears were misplaced, and as you'll read in the pages ahead, Daniel has become a part of Greg's life in a way we could have never imagined. It's said, that "God works in mysterious ways". Never have I seen that take on more meaning than in the role Daniel has played in Greg's life. We started with baby steps which included a weekly outing with Greg and Daniel. The beauty of Greg's life is that it soon became apparent that it was less important what they did together, focused more on who he was doing it with. Along the way, Daniel also introduced Greg to his family and in true Greg fashion, Dan's family became Greg's family, Dan's friends became Greg's friends. Total acceptance -- by both of these young men – what a lesson for all of us. Never have I see someone live their life by example, and have the impact Daniel has. As you'll read, other young men eventually became Greg's friends, based on an introduction from Dan. Dan's own brother Andrew also became a key member of Greg's inner circle, sharing the same warm, accepting style of Greg that Dan first started.

We had no idea that this relationship would last, or grow with the deep roots we see today. But last it has. I cannot begin to capture, the blessing of Daniel in Greg's life. Suffice to say Daniel brought us hope and happiness. Hope that a society that values perfection and image above substance, could in fact find a meaningful role for our son in the universe. Happiness, in knowing that Greg has a friend, someone who truly cares for him, even loves him, beyond his family. It may not be cool to hang with the kid with a disability – Dan has never cared.

The seed of friendship found in that pool, so many years ago, has grown into a mighty maple. The integrity of a young man named Dan, has changed Greg's life, and our lives too. In the chapter's ahead, you'll read more about this amazing young man named Daniel, and a family who has inspired him to a life of service. We watch the Rossi family – role models for all of us – and how they live their lives, in word and deed, according to the teachings of the ultimate Father. They don't preach; they do not judge; instead they embrace others with the unconditional love of a higher power and in the process, change lives!

ı Our Greg is a man now. A man with a disability. But unlike the day of his birth, when we were filled with fear and apprehension, we now know there is a plan. A plan that includes Greg changing the views of what others perceive around persons with disabilities. And he's doing that with his best friend Daniel, who has opened doors for Greg that we couldn't.

We've learned throughout this journey, that life is filled with teachers and learners.

Our Greg is a teacher and we couldn't be prouder of him. **Our** Daniel is also a teacher and we've learned so much from him about how one person can make a difference. The Lord does work in 'mysterious ways'. Regardless of the next chapter, we will be forever grateful for the mystery that brought Greg, and Daniel, into our lives.

CHAPTER ONE

FRIENDSHIP REVEALED

*I don't know what your destiny will be, but one thing I
know: the only ones among you who will be really happy
are those who will have sought and found how to serve.*

—Albert Schweitzer

Greg and the Boys in concert

How can one consolidate words that describe someone who; brings a smile to your face every time he calls – remembers the silliest things that you have done and laughs just as hard every time he retells them to you – how can you put into words the feeling you get when you sing Britney Spears as loud as you can, while waiting for a red light to turn green – learn and become part of a band that sings 'Backstreet Boys' mostly because that's what his favorite music is. How do you describe someone that loves Tim Horton's Ice Caps so much that despite the coldest day he will soon enough enjoy an ice cap over something warm. You can't verbalize how someone can love you in such a way that changes your life, re-formats your understanding of friendship and allows you to become vulnerable to a friendship that has taught me the true meaning of love. You can see how hard it is to describe such a person – there's no one way to explain to you how such a person graciously interrupted my life 12 years ago, but I will indulge you with how I came to meet, Gregory James O'Brien.

I never thought that a little boy with Down Syndrome would have such a powerful impact on my life that I would forever be grateful to him for teaching me the meaning of love, friendship and honesty.

I want it to be clear that I do not think of myself too highly or more than I ought. The reality is that I am just a man, at the end of my term on earth my body will return to dust and my soul to heaven. What makes my life special and this story worth telling is the sole fact that God, through a sequence of events, that I had no control of, allowed certain things to transpire in my life. He provided a parenting combination that has placed value on compassion and serving others and friendships that most people are afraid to have. I've been privileged to call Greg a friend and truly have received more in our friendship than what I could ever imagine giving.

WHERE ARE WE INVESTING OUR LIVES?

Before this story unfolds, I want to encourage you to ask yourself the question of where you are investing your life – how do you rank life priorities, how do you share your love with others, how do you use your life to impact others and what is important to you? What I have learned in this life is that it does no good to compare your life to another, because that will bring only disappointment. Rather, know that you have a story to tell, and that your being here is neither by chance nor randomness, but for a purpose.

Jesus' parable of the rich fool found in Luke 12:13-34 questions where we invest our best time, energy, and life priorities. Perhaps this Bible text is as good as any to consider as a challenge in our reflections on the Bible's call to end poverty.

The context leading to this is one of Jesus resisting the power brokers and the powers. Jesus had just angered the Pharisees and scholars in their own home by teaching that acceptance by God comes not from greedy lives that look clean, but generous lives shared with the poor (Luke 11:39-41); not from tithing, but justice and love: not from status seeking and exclusion, but serving (Luke 11:43-54). These power brokers were insulted and opposed Jesus fiercely. As Jesus left, a mob of many thousands gathered, so that "they trampled on one another" (Luke 12:1). Those who have been in a mob situation know that the fear can be almost tangible. Jesus drew his disciples close at that point and called them to have courage in the face of the powers of the Pharisees and scholars. God would have the ultimate say over their lives (Luke 12:2-12). A voice from someone in the crowd intervened and said, "Teacher, tell my brother to divide the family inheritance with me" (Luke 12:13). The crowd hushed, straining to hear the answer. Yet, Jesus refused to arbitrate over a dead person's possessions and moved rather to address the crowd. He warned them, "Take Care! Be on your guard against all kinds of greed; for one's life does not consist in the abundance of possessions" (Luke 12:15). This word "greed" has a negative connotation of desiring to have more, and Jesus then told the famous parable of a certain rich man who was willing to defer his happiness by building bigger and bigger barns to store his surplus grain, with the idea that one day he could take life easy, eat, drink, and be merry. But he died. God then called him a "fool," asking what he had invested his life in.

Jesus explained the point of the parable, "So it is for those who store up treasures for themselves but are not rich towards God" (Luke 12:21), and shows the folly of letting possessions like clothes, food, buildings, or careers, which are "here today and gone tomorrow," possess us.

We live in a world that does not take these warnings about greed seriously or personally. People with disabilities suffer from this form of poverty, a poverty that doesn't amount itself in monetary weakness, rather, in the form of alienation from greater society. When our lives become so busy and consumed with the everyday accounts of life and we leave no room for others, society suffers, people suffer, and we end up suffering. Some of the most beautiful moments in life come from when we share with one another in love. There are hundreds of people, thousands of people in our communities that suffer from the poverty that keeps people like you and me from sharing our lives with others, especially those that are labeled as disabled. It can be too easy to look at ourselves and make excuses – not good enough, not spiritual enough, not young enough, not old enough, not smart enough, not enough time or energy, or my favorite, when I settle down and am financially secure – that's when I can start to help others. Well let me tell you a little secret, those that need us whether as a friend, a donor, a volunteer or organizer can't justify you waiting or making excuses as to why you're not stepping up and lending a helping hand in the life of another.

I'll leave you with this reflection – and your honest answer. Now, allow me to begin my story of friendship.

CHAPTER TWO

DISABILITY EXPOSED

Do not forget to entertain strangers, for by so doing some people have entertained angels without knowing it.

Hebrews 13:2

Andrew and Greg doing their 'Titanic' Impression

I've never considered writing in such a way to share my life with others or considering my stories to be book worthy. Contrary to what I just told you I truly feel that this story that God has blessed me with is worthy of sharing with others, and for those that know me, you also know that I would not think twice about verbally recounting the story of how I met Greg O'Brien, however, before I could tell you about Greg, I need to share a couple of stories that segway my soft spot for people with disabilities.

MY FIRST ENCOUNTER

I was 14, just dropped off at the Blackdown Army Cadet training centre at Base Borden (Barrie, ON). I was embarking on a 6-week training course that was to cover field craft and survival, sports, drill, and a summer away from Mom, Dad and my brother. I didn't particularly enjoy my short time spent with the Army Cadets, albeit a grand organization that provides some form of overt discipline. I recall being withdrawn when I entered the module tent that was to be my place of rest for the six-week course. I was placed in Foxtrot Company, and immediately fell into the same routine of early morning wake up, PT or physical training that mostly comprised of a run, group marches over to the meal tent and then the structured days activities. It was like clockwork, a well oiled engine that accounted for every move, every minute of your time. The staff were only a few years older than most of the students and never failed to find their fill of people to yell at, people to make examples of and excuses to vent some form of pent-up anger at some poor soul. Like I said I was withdrawn, didn't say much, kept my bunk clean, didn't cause a stir, I don't even remember being yelled at. The module tent that I shared with 10 other boys was rowdy most of the time, and stories would go for hours-on-end at night until the eyelids became too heavy to carry and the words a slight murmur.   The stories mostly comprised of what girl was looking good and who was staking their claims in the childish game of teen romance.   Submersed in my own world at times, I would rather read from the Bible that my father left me mixed with listening to the tales of boys wanting to become men, but missing a few steps in the process.

Routine is not my thing. Soon I was waking up early to go for runs before PT, because I felt the pace was too slow for me and I wanted a work out. I was entering high school that summer and I knew that I wanted to try out for the football team and thought that a summer of running and obstacle courses would endeavor to build me up some before the football try-outs. When PT wasn't chal-lenging enough for me I woke up early and went for runs. It's amazing the energy I had looking back because now that years have passed since my days in Borden I wish I had that energy every now and then. Some mornings, if mom was lucky, I would even place a collect call from the payphone to her at the early hours of the morning. The runs I went on were magnificent, an opening to the quiet world before it was touched again by human chaos, unin-terrupted and unspoiled, it seemed that it was the rising sun that was my running companion, and I never complained.

As the camp was drawing to a near, it was custom that the staff choose one cadet out of the 140 in the company to lead them throughout the remainder of the course. The position called for that cadet to march the group from class to class, to the meal halls, to do roll call at night, and be the voice between cadet and staff. I don't know what they were looking for in the way of a resume but I found myself the leader of the Foxtrot Company for two weeks. And boy!!! Let me tell you, I went from someone who was hardly known to the most called upon person in our company lines. I started to field calls of nuisance com-plaints, girls that were upset at boys, boys that were upset at boys, and boys upset at girls. The staff shared privileged information – albeit not CIA type information, but little perks such as an extra swim, extra time off, that sort of thing. I don't know the rationale for the choice that was made to put me in charge, but I did accept it.

I think that is enough of a prelude to give you an idea of what I was involved with that summer. It was during my rule as the leader of Foxtrot Company that an event happened that would forever change my life. As the leader I ate last and if you're a leader of some kind and the occasion arises that food is on the schedule for your group, colleagues, or soldiers you make sure you eat last as well. I brought up the line that day and welcomed the meal that I had no say in on my plate. The meal tents were large and filled with other companies that were on base doing whatever course. You could imagine the amount of chatter, everyone is dressed the same and if you're not fast you may not get those little ice cream cups with the wooden spoon...or at least a second serving of one. These meal tents, and I can later testify, meal halls both in the military and at university are havens for gossip, attention seekers, cliques and boys willing to do something stupid for whatever reason.

That day I found myself walking through the tent and I couldn't find any familiar faces to sit with as I must have been in the wrong section. As I made my way down the centre aisle I passed a boy and instantly something told me that I should know him but I couldn't place him to that sense. As I passed him I could hear him asking where his friends were and if anyone had seen them. He was frantically walking with his tray and asking groups of people if they had seen his 'friends'. That boy without knowing it openly invited the ridicule from a group of all-stars (boys that think too highly of themselves) from a nearby table. I clearly heard their taunting, "Over here...Sit here loser. 'What? Can't find your friends?.....what, those glasses aren't binoculars?" I didn't tell you that the boy I passed had the largest, thickest glasses I'd had ever seen and later I found out it was because he was legally blind. At this point, some of the other tables had quieted down; generally when a dominated group is louder than the rest the masses draw their attention to the situation at hand.

I'm sure that there was someone wanting to put a stop to this foolishness that day; I just beat them to it. I went straight to the table and said, "That's enough, he's with ME!!!" I walked up to the boy and told him I would take him to his friends.

We never found his friends that day, but I did have lunch with him and cannot remember his name and truthfully cannot tell you anything else other than he was one of the 140 in Foxtrot Company. I knew I had known him from somewhere, and that day it took some time and some taunting but he found a friend to have lunch with. I had one more encounter with him, and that was when one of his lenses had popped out and he came to my tent to find me. I placed the lens back in, secured it with some tape and told him to be extra careful.

Kids can be cruel, and Mom used to tell me when I was young and crying from being bullied that "They (kids) don't realize the harm that words have on someone." That was always followed by the reassurance of "Sticks and stones can break your bones, but don't let words hurt you." Amen!!! Easier said than done right??

The rest of that summer went smooth, when camp came to an end, the withdrawn person that I was upon entering that summer became a mere glimpse of the person that was leaving the confines of CFB Borden. I had gained some courage through the leadership position bestowed on me and more importantly I was exposed to downright discrimination and ignorance that would add to a piece of my character and engrained my soul with compassion for others.

CHAPTER THREE

A STEP IN THE RIGHT DIRECTION

When your heart speaks — take good notes!

- Susan Campbell

Ethiopian Sunset

There was definitely something different about me when I had left CFB Borden. Before I entered grade 9 I wanted to find out more about people with disabilities – I had developed a soft spot for those I did not know how to engage, for those I did not know how to speak to, for those that kids and adults would shun and use words such as 'RETARD' and "There's something wrong with that kid' or my favorite, 'He must have some kind of mental problem.' Oh how easy it is to label and deflect with some unintelligent words. I saw something different when I saw someone with an intellectual disability or a physical disability, I saw a story, I saw survival, I saw a resilience that goes beyond my understanding, I saw, and still see, life in all its beauty manifested in those that we deem less fortunate.

Being 14 and calling organizations in the Markham area to volunteer with youth and adults with intellectual disabilities was quite difficult. Despite my sincerity and persistence I kept being shut down from various organizations. They would tell me to come back in a few years and try again at that point. Well.... you'll have to know that I am one of the least patient men when it comes to waiting in these types of endeavors. Fortunately enough, a social worker called from one of the organizations that I had continually harassed. The stars must have aligned that day, because she had told me of a young man in her care whose mother was looking for someone to take him out, be friends with and play sports!! Without hesitation, I said 'YES!'

For the purposes of confidentiality I will resort to the use of 'John' for the boy that I met the few weeks prior to the start of grade 9. John was 19 years old and I never wanted to ask in my naivety at the time what was wrong with him. I told you that this was not a verifiable way to inquire about someone, by asking what is wrong with them...so naturally that was the first thing I asked. However, this was prior to my current philosophy of people being wonderfully intricate in their creation. John had red birthmarks on the entire left side of his body, including his face. In addition, the left side of his body had been affected by a stroke at a young age and he never regained proper functioning; it was underdeveloped and limited in range of movement.

John lived close to Markham Main St. and the kind social worker that set up our first meeting, accompanied me to his residence the day we met. I will quickly admit that I was nervous beyond belief! I remember walking up the stairs to their apartment. I remember standing in their living room, meeting John's mom, his older sister, and having a drink of water. The social worker and John's mom chatted like old friends, and I just sat there. I tried not to stare at John's physical appearance and wondered what we would do or if we could be friends at all. I was scared that I wouldn't know the slightest thing to do, or what to say. John quickly broke that barrier and asked if I wanted to play basketball. From that moment on there would never be an awkward feeling between the two of us. So we played basketball, and I was so impressed that a guy, who only had legitimately one strong side of his body functioning, was pretty darn good at basketball. Even though John was older than me, and disabled, he taught me the importance of using your imagination. I think John knew that we could never play one-on-one against each other – John was disabled not stupid, and he knew that I would let him pass without playing hard defense or pretending to miss an open shot. To compensate for the lack of competition, John had us playing against the two best basketball players at that time, Michael Jordan and Scotty Pippen, from the Chicago Bulls. The way it worked was simple, first you needed an imagination second, for every miss we had it was a point for them, we still had to play as if one of them were defending us and try to elude their impenetrable defense. I'll admit, at first it was a little out of my league to imagine playing against NBA pro's, but after a couple of games I taught myself to become vulnerable around John. It's interesting; society teaches us to be on our guard, and not to trust anyone. My time with the Canadian Armed Forces Reserves and as a police officer, taught me to air with a side of caution, don't give up too much of yourself to others, maintain 360 degrees of observation and constantly maintain situational awareness. I became vulnerable, and that is a technique that has allowed me to enjoy some of the best friendships I could have ever imagined. Through becoming vulnerable I enjoyed the basketball games just as much as John, I would get frustrated when Jordan and Pippen would score when either of us missed, I was a part of the excitement that John had when he drove the lane and threw up a left-handed layout and acted as if he had just dunked right over Pippen's head! Conversely, I think of what would have happened if I did not allow myself to become vulnerable? I probably would have had a fake smile on my face and pretended to enjoy myself as I convinced my body that I was serving humanity and actively making a difference in some kid's life! I am so thankful that I learnt at a young age to choose the latter, and feel the difference being made when you become someone's friend and not just some feel good helper!

EVERYTHING HAS A REASON

Train a child in the way he should go, and
when he is old he will not turn from it.

- ***Proverbs 22:6 -***

You know I didn't just wake up one day and decide to share my life with those less fortunate. Life is about call and response – you are called by God's grace into different situations and your response is the character-defining component of your life.

Dad, or to most that know him, Joe Rossi is quite the man, very humble and wise and has spent his whole life leading by example. Not a bad role model for my brother and me growing up.

When Andrew and I were young, mom and dad's world was turned upside down through circumstances that my parents could not control. We were young but could remember when our parents had to file for bankruptcy. We were victims of circumstance and when you become a victim of any crime you are left vulnerable and helpless. Hindsight is such a valuable tool for putting pieces of the puzzle together and making sense of what we perceive at times to be the most difficult times of our lives. I don't want to underestimate challenging times in our life, we all have them, we all have struggles, and despite their difficulty, we survive and thankfully can learn from these encounters. When my family went bankrupt that started the constant moving from different rental homes, basements, and town homes – constantly searching for our next place to live that was reasonably in budget. It meant that Andrew and I would switch schools, never being able to really find a solid group of friends throughout our elementary schooling. Both of us would be the culprits of child injustice. Mom would take us shopping at the *Salvation Army Thrift Store*, which comprised of our wardrobe at the time from grade 5 to grade 9 for both Andrew and I. It's most unfortunate but when in elementary school when you wear things that aren't within the current fad you are quickly singled out. Ripped jeans and Nike were the fashion of my elementary school years...and my blue jeans with suede back pockets were the single worst pair of pants I could have ever worn. I was ridiculed so much because of those things I truly did not wear or purchase another pair of jeans until I was in my first year of University. My summer attire consisted of some ratty tie-dyed shirt (which I truly liked) and black bike shorts; items that found myself running home at lunch so I could escape the rampant insults of kids not realizing the power of their words.

Dad had to work two jobs, mom was working retail and Andrew and I had two paper routes, in addition, we would wash cars in summer and shovel driveways in winter for $2.00. And that was a steal, Andrew now has his own private company that does snow removal in the winter and I can assure you – having worked for him he no longer charges $2.00 for a driveway. Mom and Dad worked hard and endeavored to make time for us – our family time comprised of board games such as 'Monopoly, Sorry and Hungry Hippo.' Mom and Dad would take Andrew and me for drives when they both had the time off. And When Mom knew that we wouldn't see Dad for days, Mom would take us to the fire department where Dad worked (Dad has just received his 25 year of Service Medal from the Markham Fire Department). Andrew and I would play basketball with the crew, dad would always get us to help him out with washing the truck and we could dream of being a firefighter, just like dad. Mom would bring food for Dad's crew and Mom has always had been a good cook, and that was a large part of how we spent time as a family.

Dad would always refer life lessons back to the Bible and how important it was for Andrew and me to live our lives the way Jesus has asked us to. Mom and Dad would always tell us to look after widows and orphans, and to be nice to the poor. I couldn't grasp what that meant since we were poor, there was no way that we as a family could help any widow or orphan, and plus I didn't even think I knew any! Mom and Dad were determined that they teach their children that it doesn't matter how much money you have, Jesus himself lived below His means. What mattered the most was how you shared the time that God has given you with others and how your time shared with another is more valuable than any amount of riches.

It was the first snow fall of the year, and 15 years ago Ontario would get wicked snowfalls and 'snow days' were very common – not so much anymore, but it seemed like we would get 4-5 snow days a year at that time! Mom woke us up around 3 o'clock in the morning; at the time I was in grade 5 and Andrew in grade 4. Three in the morning was way too early and we really had no idea what was going on when Mom got us dressed, told us to eat something, gave us a glass of milk and pushed us out the door. Dad was outside, the driveway was already shoveled and the Big Black truck that served as our only vehicle was already running. Dad piled us in the truck and didn't field any of the questions that we asked him...'what is going on!!!' Dad just drove; it didn't take long for us to arrive at our final destination. That destination was at Grandma Agnes' house. Grandma Agnes was a widow whose husband was shot and killed in Jamaica and she had moved her family to Canada afterwards to raise her two daughters, who actually ending up babysitting us from time to time.

So there's at least three feet of snow, it's early and we were standing in Grandma Agnes' driveway! Dad told us to be very quiet and not to make too much noise, he handed us a shovel each and the three of us went off to work. Dad didn't want Grandma Agnes to wake, nor did he want her to know who had shoveled her driveway. Dad told Andrew and me that day that God sees the works you do in secret and His rewards are greater than you could ever imagine. I'm sure that Grandma Agnes knew who was shoveling her driveway, but she never said or named anyone, she would always say that 'Angels' would come and clear her driveway for her. That's the best part of the story – Love became manifested in our actions and had nothing to do with our wallets. Andrew and I learned that it is more powerful and longer lasting when you share of yourself and invest time in making someone else feel special.

DAD, THE SERVANT LEADER

That Christmas, two things happened that would set the course of how my family would give to others for the next 20 years. The first was a day trip to the Eaton Centre downtown. One of Dad's jobs was being security at the Sheraton Hotel in Toronto and they had a Cineplex attached to their location at the time. Mom would bring us down and somehow we always got to watch movies for free! So we were walking around the Eaton Centre and for a little guy it's a pretty neat experience, I remember that there were more people walking around than I had ever seen before, crowding stores and people spending money. The only money that we would be spending was on lunch that day and boy we were getting hungry. Andrew and I have been known for our appetites and when hunger strikes, man does it ever strike. Mom and Dad led us to the food court of the Eaton Centre and luckily enough we found a little four-seat table for our lunch. Mom went up to get us some food, and dad disappeared. Mom came back with a tray of food and dad was still nowhere to be found. Mom knew what was going on, but I had no clue. Mom insisted that we started to eat, which for our family is unusual, we were taught to wait until everyone is seated before we start to eat, and dad was still nowhere to be found. So we started to eat and just as we were enjoying our food I saw my father walking down the escalator towards to the food court at the Eaton Centre. The unusual thing about what was going on was that there was a homeless guy following dad! At first I thought the worst, dad was going to be robbed or the guy might jump my dad. As they made their way through the crowd, dad turned to the man shared some words and it became apparent that they were together. Dad walked and his friend followed, vividly I remember crowds would part as they approached, at this point I had stopped eating and was watching dad's actions. I was confused, here was my dad who was supposed to have lunch with his family, at no point did he tell us what he was doing and now people were looking at the two of them, making faces and getting out of the way as if they both have some incurable communicable airborne disease!

They walked straight up to the McDonalds' line-up and went straight to the front of the line. Dad turned to ask what the gentleman would like to eat and made the order, I saw him pull his wallet, pay for the bill, grab the tray and then lead his friend through the crowds looking for an open table. Dad didn't have to look for long before he found a spot that two people conveniently were leaving at the same time my dad and estranged friend stood beside their table. Dad sat down with the man, and dad then handed the man one bag containing the lunch that my father was supposed to have with us. I remember being embarrassed for my father and it was probably because I was young and couldn't understand what my father was doing. Dad sat there as his friend ate the entire lunch dad provided, dad had nothing to eat that day but listened to whatever stories that homeless man decided to share with dad. Dad did come back to our table; the man he left was still at the table enjoying the atmosphere of the busy Eaton Centre. Dad didn't say anything; we just picked up our belongings and made our departure.

It would be six years to the date that I witnessed my father perform such an act when I would understand why he did what he did that day in the Eaton Centre. I've always been an observant person and this particular memory has never escaped my mind.

I was in grade eleven and on a field trip with my economics class we went to the Toronto Stock Exchange for the day. When it came to lunchtime I was searching for a feasting hole with my friends. We had an hour and there were multiple places to choose from to enjoy a quick meal. McDonalds was the place of choice. As I was walking towards the golden arches I saw a homeless guy sitting outside and I had a rush of memory come back to me about what my father did six years earlier. The streets of Toronto were packed and I froze, right outside of McDonalds having a battle in my mind about whether to ask this guy if he wants to eat lunch with me. I was 16 and felt like I was standing there for minutes debating, re-living the memory of people staring at my father, making faces – moving out of the way and why on earth had he given up his lunch for a man he didn't know. The battle in my mind was pulling me in different directions and then it happened. I knelt down and asked 'Sir, would you like some lunch today?' It just came out, nothing like I had planned and I was extremely shocked by his response 'I thought you'd never ask!' At that very moment the world stopped around me, this man accompanied me into the McDonalds and as we walked up to the counter, there were no stares, no faces being made, we bypassed the line – walked by my friends and placed our order. We found a seat and were by our-selves and that is when it all made sense to me. I never spoke to dad about that day six years ago when he gave up his lunch for a stranger. Here I was, giving up my meal for a stranger, considered an outcast by society and not caring about what was going on around me and ignoring any comments or inappropriate stares because he was a person and that is how I saw this man.

I sat there as this man ate his lunch, my friends were across the way and I listened to all the stories this man chose to share that day. Whether they were true or not, I listened, and when it was time to leave I thanked him for his time. Only one of my friends that day made any mention to me about the encounter and it was something along the lines of 'that was nice what you did.' I ate like a champ that night for dinner and was thankful that my parents who lead by example and stepped out of their comfort zone to teach Andrew and me about the magic of sharing your life with another.

CHAPTER FIVE

A CHRISTMAS I'LL NEVER FORGET

Being unwanted, unloved, uncared for, forgotten by everybody, I think that is a much greater hunger, a much greater poverty than the person who has nothing to eat.

- Mother Theresa

The Rossi Family

Let me retreat back a little bit. Grade 5 – family is bankrupt – Andrew and I were ridiculed at school for wearing the same clothes all the time, we had no money. To my best estimation in grade 5 you have to be around 10 or 11. It was the same year that dad had lunch with the homeless guy downtown Toronto. That Christmas was one of the most special Christmas' I will ever remember. I told you that two things happened that changed how my family operated for the next 20 years. Christmas Day, Dad was working and we chose to open presents after dad was home from work. We were renting a town house that year and Andrew and I would keep ourselves occupied playing 'Lego wars' a game we made up and when we became bored of that we played floor stick hockey. Mom was cooking dinner and finishing up with her baking when we heard the distinct noise of our black truck pulling into the driveway. When Dad came through the door he had a large black garbage bag slung over his shoulder. Dad was still in his uniform and brought the bag up the flight of stairs into our living room and placed it on the ground in front of us. Mom and Dad were both sad that Christmas because they weren't able to buy Andrew or me any gifts, and in return Andrew or I couldn't provide any gifts for our parents. We drafted up a bunch of coupons that year for house cleaning and truck washing, I even offered to vacuum the house, something that I hated when I was a kid. There we were with this giant garbage bag at our feet and dad was saying a prayer for thankfulness. He then emptied the bag onto the floor revealing all of its contents, and 'My O My' did Christmas ever come! There were various gifts from stuffed animals to G.I. Joe figurines to board games!! Andrew and I were excited to say the least, and as every kid on Christmas Day, we couldn't wait to play with all the new gifts we had just received!

Never again would we have a Christmas like that one! For the 20 years that followed that Christmas my family would not be isolated and empty handed with no gifts to share with each other. The very next year, Mom and Dad started volunteering at the local Salvation Army Food Bank. Dad used to clean the offices of the food-bank every month and during the Christmas season they wanted to volunteer their time. I was in grade 6, and I remember Mom pulled Andrew and me out of school two days before the Christmas Holiday started. That's exciting, being pulled out early for a two-week holiday was just what every kid wanted.

So there we were the Rossi family putting food hampers together for underprivileged families. If you've never been into a Christmas warehouse it is quite the production. There are shelves upon shelves of food, and mountains of every toy you could think of, stuffed animals to the newest in electronics, make-up for girls and my all time favorite, LEGO!

Having seen all of the toys as an 11 year old boy, I of all people would fit the description of a Santa's helper who would put packages together for kids whose parents couldn't afford toys that Christmas. Naturally when I was told that I would be working in the food packaging area I was distraught!!! I did accept my position and until the very day that we retired from running the Salvation Army Food Bank I never packed a single toy request for a child! Andrew and I were the food and toy runners – that was literally our job description for 20 years, we had loads of older ladies that would graciously give of their time every year without fail and they would pack hampers of food and bags of toys to be distributed to families that were waiting everyday for handouts. I would always carry the food hampers for the first couple of years, which was probably the last time that I was bigger and stronger than Andrew. Depending on the family size would determine the amount of food hampers that they would receive, and if that family had any children then their kids filled out a 'Christmas wish list' and would hopefully receive something that they had asked for. Distribution took place over a period of six days, families had to fill out an application to receive food and toys two months prior and then they were given a distribution day to come gather their allotted provisions.

This is how it worked! The Santa's helpers in the back of the warehouse under Mom's direction would put together food hampers and toy bags, each were numbered and had a subsequent name on them. Andrew and I would take the packages from the back to a staging area where we would place the food and toys in numerical order for the next day's pick-up. Pick-up days were scheduled two days apart from each other so the women in the back had enough time to sort everything out for the hundreds of families that would be visiting throughout the Christmas season. A member of a family would come present their application, which had their assigned pick-up number and wait until Andrew and I brought their allotment forward. 90% of the time it was women that would come to pick up the food and toy provisions. I soon realized that this was because it was difficult for men to come to a place where essentially they were saying 'I need help, I cannot provide food for my family or toys for my children!' It is damaging to men to become so vulnerable, so their wives would come on the family's behalf.

Andrew and I would bring the food hampers and bag of toys straight to people's cars or the awaiting taxis outside. Our fingers would become raw from picking up the cardboard hampers and the knotted garbage bags filled with toys. Once we placed the items in the vehicles we would always wish people a 'Merry Christmas'. Andrew and I were exposed to a subversive form of poverty, hidden from the eye of the general public. People would show up empty and leave with a form of hope and appreciation. Andrew and I would go on to receive hundreds of thank-you's. We saw people at their lowest spectrum of life, having to receive the basic necessities of life because they could not provide them for their families. Thousands of tears would litter the parking lot, as we would pile food and toys into the awaiting cars. Andrew and I knew that we were the same age as some of the children that were receiving gifts and food. We had access to their applications as they were handed to us to find the hamper and toy bag that was particularly prepared for their family – free from foods that they could not eat or were allergic to and toy bags that had gifts close to, if not exactly, what they were hoping for. The applications had the age of the kids. There was one mother who came to pick up her provisions who had three kids at home all around Andrew's and my age. I remember the large beat up Astro Van that she arrived in. As we started to bring out the hampers and toy bags and wishing her a Merry Christmas, Andrew turned to me and said there was another toy bag that he had to go and get. This lady was so thankful, and thanked us as we packed up her van. I mentioned that Andrew had another toy bag for her, and judging from the hockey sticks poking out of the giant black garbage bag as Andrew slung it over his shoulder and struggled to carry it out, that was exactly what her kids were asking for. She began to cry. When she gained control of her tears she thanked us and said, 'I won't have time to wrap all these toys, and I'll just have to give these bags to my kids to open up.' At that moment it made sense, Andrew and I were cheerfully bringing food hampers and toy bags out to cars that we had failed to realize that the same giant black garbage bags filled with toys that Andrew would carry is the same garbage bag that Dad had brought home for us to open only last year. It was only a year prior that we, my family were a recipient of the same kindness from the food bank. It became clear, we knew what those kids were in for when the bag of toys was emptied on their floor and a parent would quietly whisper thank you to God for providing toys for their children that year.

As I mentioned we ran the food bank for 20 years after this and each year, Andrew and I would be pulled out of school early, and start the process of making people's Christmas by donating the most precious commodity and the thing that we all have in abundance, our time!

CHAPTER SIX

SEEKING DISABILITIES

*I am a little pencil in the hand of a writing God
who is sending a love letter to the world.*

- Mother Theresa

After having the opportunity of working with John and defeating Michael Jordan and Scotty Pippen on numerous fictitious encounters I still wanted to do more for people living with disabilities.

I'm Italian through and through, I mean 100% of the real stuff and as you can imagine when it comes to work what are Italian's main occupation??? Construction!!! Well I'll have to admit we were no different. Coming out of Bankruptcy Dad no longer had three jobs. He had two! With his days off from the fire department he was able to open up his own small business construction company and had the hardest workers, his two sons. Dad specialized on foundation repairs otherwise known as leaky basements. One of the on-going jokes in my family is that Dad never believed in machines and nor should he since his sons were little excavators that could dig a hole at best within an hour. Plus, machines made a mess and dad was all about his final product looking as close to the way we found it before we dug down to someone's foundation wall in order to repair a water crack.

Working for Dad had more benefits than I could count; the biggest was that Mom would make lunch for us everyday without fail. Despite the comfort of a summer under Dad's supervision I asked Dad in the summer of 1996 if he would allow me to go and work for a day camp as a one-on-one councillor for children with disabilities. It was a significant pay reduction from the $20.00 an hour that dad was paying me (and if you have ever worked at a day camp then you know that you are extremely close to volunteering your time in comparison to what they pay you!).

Markham Day Camp, Day One!! I was matched up with a young boy that had a degenerative disability. A degenerative disability is just that, Mark was only 12 years old and according to his mother in his short life he had lost his ability to communicate, use his fine and gross motor skills which reduced him to a wheel chair 90% of the time and cognitively the same digression was apparent. Mark had no control of his bowel movements and was in diapers – which for me meant that I had to learn well beyond my parenting years to change, clean and place on diapers!

At that time, Markham day camps integrated children with disabilities into everyday activities and programs with the mainstream campers. There was a dozen or so staff who were my colleagues working directly with children with exceptionalities. Mark's mother had prepared me graciously to work with her son. I met Mark prior to the start of camp and was introduced to what Mark liked and didn't like, and the activities that he preferred to play.

This had been for me the second time at someone's house in which I was meeting a child I was going to spend a significant amount of time with, and I still felt awkward and silent.

By no means am I a shy person, I have the ability to involve myself in some significant extroverted moments. A brief one I will quickly share was when I was kicked out of an Esso gas station in Guelph Ontario for dancing while filling up gas. In all truthfulness my dancing escapades that day were nothing but normal for citizens that regularly fill up their vehicles at service stations. This song from the blockbuster Shrek started playing on the stereo, and my buddy Marcel who was in the driver's seat turned up the volume, and it quickly struck a chord through my soul and what happened during the next four minutes of my life I cannot recall; except for the fact that when the song was over, I had developed a brow of sweat, a slight retreat of air and looks from the numerous customers who all had bewildered faces. As I went back to the nozzle inserted into the truck, the attendant greeted me over the loud speaker by asking me to pack my things, don't worry about paying and please leave immediately. Shocked, yet elated, I didn't put up a fight when I noticed that the gas meter read $10.00, and since I was asked to leave without paying, I wondered if I did this sort of thing more often if I would get free gas regularly.

Despite the fact that I have the natural ability to be outgoing, I have always suffered when I have met the moth-

ers of the numerous children that I have worked with –
I become silent, awkward and feeling like I'm not selling
myself as this kind hearted person that they can entrust
the care of their child under.

I can remember that the first thing Mark got really
excited over was playing ball – which he had enough
motor skill to sit on his backside with legs extended out,
I would mirror his position with my feet touching his and
we would pass the ball back and forth. This would come
to be the game that we would play the most during that
summer. The second thing that I remember was that Mark
had a little sister at least six years his junior and instantly I
knew that despite her young age she was more mature
than some of the adults I know when it comes to dealing
with people living with exceptionalities. Her care and loving approach to Mark was something to marvel at for me,
she was a leader without knowing it, an inspiration without
having to give a presidential speech! She would become
one of my mentors that I would learn from during that summer, and she was only seven.

The way that camp worked was that parents would
choose the different locations, which offered different programs for their children. Each camp had a distinct special program for the various interests of the children that
attended, and ran for two weeks in duration. Mark and his
sister were signed up for three different camps that summer.
Our first posting was at Markville Secondary School that was
close to where I lived. I was glad when I arrived for work that
a good friend of mine was working with a boy in a wheelchair and we would be together for the first two weeks!

I would do my best to incorporate Mark into the programs that the other children were involved with. It was
always difficult, most of the programs were movement ori-
entated, which made it interesting to say the least. I would
do a dance routine with Mark as he was in his wheelchair –
I thought it looked good and I would spin him around or
dance around him, which always brought a smile to his face.

It didn't take long before the biggest question that I
would field that summer from campers and staff alike when

it came to Mark was – 'What's wrong with him (Mark)? Most of the kids would ask me, and the ones that didn't would ask one of the other camp councillors and I would often overhear their answer, 'I don't know.'

The sad fact is that adults ask the same questions when they come across someone with an exceptionality, they ask what's wrong with that person miles before they recognize that indeed that person is a person and has a name. It seems that few of us remember our social etiquette and when we come into contact with a person with an exceptionality we ask what's wrong with that person before we even ask their name! I find that even when you answer the question of what is wrong with that person (whoever it is) the answer is often not understood or they are totally unaware of that particular condition. There's many ways to label those with exceptionalities, the common ones you will hear are, "They're slow", "They are not all there in the head," "they were born dumb." The label that existed between all ages and the one that I loathe the most is, "They are retarded." To label people retarded was mainstream starting in the early 40's, and unfortunately it has stuck. People have been labeled retarded since I could remember as a kid growing up and I still find adults today use the word freely, sometimes followed with a question as to what is the politically proper way of describing this marginalized group. I can't stand the word 'retard' I refuse to use the word in any reference and take offence when I overhear the word used in an inappropriate manner, or especially when used to refer to a person. The actual word 'retard' as defined by the Webster's dictionary means, "to make slow; delay the development or progress of (an action, process, etc.); hinder or impede." The dictionary goes on to include the slang version of the word which includes, "Slang: Disparaging – a. a mentally retarded person – b. a person who is stupid, obtuse, or ineffective in some way: a hopeless social retard." It is amazing that we have incorporated this label into contemporary dictionaries that describe people in our society. There is an injustice here and as you read this book I encourage you to continually reflect on how you can change your outlook on people with exceptionalities if you haven't already.

Besides calling people 'retarded' the next thing that irks me is when people feel the need to act out their version of a 'retarded' person. It mostly looks like this – you curl your hands towards each other, suck your lips into your mouth, contort you face and speak in an audible yet slow, almost unintelligent tone.

At the time of writing this book I am 28 years old and I still witness this obscene act from people my age and older.

I acknowledge that as a society we have made leaps and bounds in how we care for and integrate people with exceptionalities. Slowly social activist groups are closing down the walls of institutions that have horrendously housed and completely isolated people with exceptionalities from society for decades. But, I tell you this it is not enough. Everyday people living with exceptionalities climb a mountain, and that mountain is overcoming the injustice being served on them by the general public, who at the core has a very small interest in the lives of those that make this climb. It's not enough to be satisfied with the status quo of allowing 'them' into the public sphere. We need to recognize that people with exceptionalities are people first, and have a multitude of skill and love that they can share with us if we give them a chance. We will discuss later about the difference that can be made.

Now take a moment and if you don't have a sibling or family member with an exceptionality when was the last time that you came across someone that could be considered 'retarded?' What were your actions? What were your thoughts? Now that we are integrating people with exceptionalities into society more and more does the term 'out of sight out of mind' keep you comforted? As any social injustice issue, there are some that are quite content living the way they do, free from external social concern. Some of us are still held up at the 'what's wrong stage' and have a hard time seeing past that.

That was quite the tangent! Now back to Mark. I was deathly afraid of the first time that I would have to change

Mark's diaper!!! I was 16 years old, reasonably in my innocence with at least 15 years before I would have to take
the responsibility on of diaper changing. Yet, here I was,
the first day of camp with Mark, and he had needed his
diaper changed! 2 hours to go before his mom picked him
up for the day and I was distraught – 'Why couldn't you
wait, Mark'. I knew that I couldn't leave it for his mother,
and besides when you have to go...you have to go!

Thank God that my good friend was working with me
that day and thank God that the child that was under
his care needed a diaper change at the same time! This
was the first diaper changing for both of usand what a
spectacle it became. There we were in the change room,
with the raw stink of feces and no fresh air. We didn't
know where to start? Our first priority was to go find surgi-
cal gloves. So I held watch as I counted on my friend to
make a speedy return. After seven minutes I was becoming impatient! There were first aid kits all over the place
and yet it was taking him what felt like forever. I started
to conspire that he went for fresh air and forgot all about
me. Finally he returned and held up one pair of gloves...
one glove for each of us! Unbelievable, it was like we had
two hands with two different minds when we started the
taking off process of the first diaper. Everything had to be
discussed prior to its execution. First diaper was off, and
I needed fresh air – I sprinted out into the gym adjacent
to the change room that we were in, straight through the
exit doors and then outside! I collected myself for round
two of the extravaganza and re-entered the diaper battlefield. Now, neither of us had any experience changing
diapers, and our first experience happened to be with two
fairly large 13-year-old boys, and we had two hands with
two different minds doing all the work. The whole process
was different for us; it took me a while to figure out which
way the diaper properly went on. When I was interviewed
for this position and they asked if I would have any difficulty changing diapers and at the time I said 'no', I didn't
realized how difficult it could have been. My first diaper
change took 45 minutes, and that day when our diaper

changing entourage left the change room, most of the other councillors gave us a standing ovation for our efforts.

By the end of the summer I would have mastered the diaper change down to minutes from first scent of poop smell to fresh diaper on. Our fellow colleagues knew of the trauma that we went through that first day and the fact that we had one glove apiece, so they gave us a 'golden glove' award for our efforts, which was a con-struction paper certificate with a spray painted gold surgi-cal glove that was glued below the accolades.

I would love to tell you that all things with Mark went smooth and that I was the most patient and faultless aid worker, but that would be a lie. I was frustrated at times when we couldn't join the other activities being played by the campers and had to settle for floor ball toss, which I described earlier to you. Mark had a reaction to sun-light and couldn't stay outside too long or he would get extremely burnt, and I love the outdoors, fresh air and just being outside; a luxury that Mark unfortunately could not enjoy as readily as you or I could. Mark and I would be outside for a few minutes and I could see the discomfort start to form in his face and knew that these moments wouldn't last long. So floor ball toss it was again! Now if you could imagine both of us on our backsides, feet extended out, soles of our shoes touching and passing the ball back and forth, you might imagine that after an hour it might get a tad tedious. It was hard for Mark to pass the ball within the diamond boundary of our legs and feet, and 70% of his passes would leave that boundary and the ball would travel wherever it felt in the gymnasium. That would require me to get up...go fetch the ball.... sit back down...re-acquire my position...and start over.... and then it would happen again...and the same process could eas-ily be repeated time and time again. I would get impa-tient having to stand up all the time to get the ball and drag my feet as I went to retrieve the ball.

Meal-time was another struggling aspect for me at times. Mark would get the best lunches packed for him by his mother. Lunch-time would start with a world of frenzy

41

from the kids around, it was like a mini Christmas at times as kids would open their lunch bags and find what was inside. I would start lunch the same way, everyday. The bib was the first thing to be put on, and that was so much easier than the diapers by far. After the bib I would hand feed Mark the different meals prepared for him. Now, I'm a veteran when it comes to eating, eating is something that I don't joke around with and take very seriously. Ever since working in the military I have made a conscious effort to eat after those that are under my leadership. So, I would always eat after Mark. Most days it went well.... but the days that it took a wrong turn, it definitely took a wrong turn! For whatever reason Mark would not be satisfied with me feeding him. I felt as though I was a new parent with a newborn and no matter what I did I could not get the baby to stop crying. Mark would wail... and I couldn't figure out why...I mean, if he was at all as hungry as I was he'd want to eat and not cry his way through lunch. I would try everything those days. You name it, I tried it, the airplane, the bunny hop to the mouth, the gentle force, the whisper talking about how good it is – a handful of times I would even try the food and hold a super happy face trying to provoke a similar reaction. Nothing!! I was 16 at the time, and after exhausting all these approaches, impatience would set in. It was times like this that I wished that I worked with some of the other kids that were high functioning disabled children. It seemed as if their councillors never had a problem during mealtime. I would be at my wits end, it was apparent to those around me and every time that I would fall from grace, an angel would come and save my day. This angel came in a small form and never failed to rescue me during these times of utmost frustration. It was Mark's sister. Without fail she would show up, and with her gentle and loving touch calm Mark down and persuade him to eat. It was her presence and love that would do the trick, she was so patient and calm that it radiated to both Mark and me and she would end up putting both of us at peace. It was an amazing thing to experience, a seven year old that would leave her spot with her friends and feed her brother and then sit with the two of us for the remainder of lunch. Lunch wasn't the only time that Mark's sister would save me. She could see when I would grow impatient, especially during floor ball toss and quickly come to my rescue yet again. With excitement she would fetch the ball if it escaped our control and hurry back to place it down in her brother's lap! During our short walks outside she would help apply sunscreen lotion to Mark's exposed skin, she would make sure that he had his hat on, and always make sure that Mark was never left alone. I witnessed so much beauty and leadership from this little girl. To me, Mark's sister manifested the verse in the Bible that reads, "I was humbled by her actions and learned the value of what love at its roots looks like." She didn't have to come to my rescue, she could have stayed with her friends who didn't see the beauty in her actions and she would comment on how she always 'played' with her brother. I marveled that at such a young age Mark's sister didn't react to other people's comments and did what she thought was right. Her actions could arguably hinder some of her friendships growing up, because some of her friends I'm sure wouldn't have understood, but she was walking away with life skills much more tangible and real than most of us ever get to experience. Love beyond words and manifested through action.

The rest of that summer went smooth; I'd like to say that my diaper skills got extremely better...but that would be an overstatement! Mark and I found ourselves at a local pool sitting in the baby pool as the rest of the kids from camp were jumping, diving and splashing around the larger swimming pool. I had known Mark at this point for about a month now and was thinking that we had a good system down, I was starting to pick up on his little quirks and he mine. Except that day I made a very rookie mistake that would cost me insurmountable damage control and quick reaction. Baby pools are notorious for being pee havens; I still think that the reason why they are warmer than the regular pool is because it's warmed by the pee that the little ones add to its waters! In the same breath of air you can't trust adults not to pee in a pool and be of the mentality that osmosis dissipates the severity of peeing in a body of water. It really is wrong in so many ways isn't it? Although, that being said I'm sure that we (me included) have had our fair share of peeing in pools. Unbeknownst to me at the time I didn't realize that the different diaper that Mark's mom pack that day was meant for swimming purposes, who knew that they made special diapers for when you go swimming! My question is, do they have them for geriatric patients for when they do water therapy? Anyway, there we are sitting in the baby pool when I noticed some bubbles coming from Mark's backside!! Now, common sense would tell you that you don't need to pull back on the back waistband to check the extent of the damage. Well, that's what I did that day, and for the women reading this, some men really do things without a logical answer for their actions! The second I pulled the waistband back a barrage of brown submarines came rushing to the surface! Baby pools are small, there happened to be approximately 10 kids and 2 councilors in the pool that day. First initial response was to save Mark and myself from the invaders... but then there were the other kids, they were totally blindsided, I yelled for the kids to evacuate the pool... it didn't take long before everyone noticed the bio-hazard that was now floating in the middle of the pool. After I secured Mark in his wheel chair I turned to see the last occupant in the pool paralyzed and not knowing what to do. It's a traumatic experience, I re-entered the danger zone, scooped the last little one up and leaped out. What was I thinking!!! I've never seen a pool lock down before that day, and I didn't even try to give testimony as to what I was thinking. I was dreading Mark's mom finding out, unpreventable because kids happen to be so honest and I knew Mark's sister would share the story right away. Two remarkable things happened that day. Mark's mother wasn't that upset, but that's my

44

perception. And the second was that I learned that they make diapers solely for swimming and that those are the ones that must be worn when a child is going into a public body of water.

CHAPTER SEVEN

HOW I MET GREG

'Daniel'!!! 'You know what I call you?
BIG SEXY'

- Greg O'Brien

At summer's end, Mark and his sister went on a family vacation and I was left jobless in a sense, I no longer had a child to care for, but I was still employed by the Town of Markham as a day camp councillor. I was re-assigned to a sport camp with a bunch of hyperactive children. I thought that this was more of my thing but these kids required a whole bunch of energy that I didn't want to extend 8 hours a day! In addition, since most of these councillors at the sport camp had worked with each other all summer they had formed their own cliques and tight circle of friends that I didn't feel as though I truly fit in. You would think that the whole 'new guy' mentality would play in my favor. You know, the new guy gets all the attention, especially from the girl councillors, or possibly from the kids...but that didn't seem to work in my favor at all. I actually felt left out, and more of a nuisance than anything, and further I missed the company of Mark and his sister.

Sometimes when you get into a routine and then have it taken away from you, it's easy to feel lost and marginalized.

The break from Mark made me ask some self reflecting questions about how his life and his sister's life had touched mine and who would have noticed that he was gone? Did anyone even notice him when he was around, and if they did what were their thoughts? I told you that Mark was suffering from a degenerative disease that eventually would claim his life, a tragedy that would result in his parents outliving him and I am sure that no parent wants to outlive their children. Mark could no longer verbally communicate, but that didn't mean to me that he couldn't understand. His sister was able to calm him down at times and get him to eat when he wouldn't, so that tells me that he could feel love, and if he could feel love then he could feel when he wasn't being loved! How many, kids that summer and councillors didn't even notice Mark? How many of them tried to engage Mark in some form of interaction? I could tell you that it wasn't many at all! This reflection made me make a conscious decision not to make that same error of not noticing those that are less fortunate, especially those with exceptionalities.

The sport camp seemed to drag on; I eventually connected with some councillors and kids and didn't feel so isolated and introverted. The sports camp had a twice a week swim schedule at Morgan Pool in Markham. Morgan Pool is fairly large and has a wicked diving board in the deep end of the pool that kids and councillors alike would try to impress the crowds with double summersaults and a variety of twist dives. The majority of their efforts resulted in awkward landings or the more painful landing of belly flops, which would always stir a response from those watching.

Our swim time was consistent with the warmest part of the day, which was a pleasant relief from the heat. Multitudes of kids would swim the waters and create havoc in and around the pool. It's kind of a nightmare when you have dozens upon dozens of kids splashing around. The chaos is remarkable, towels are lost, councillors struggle to keep kids together, making sure no one is running on the deck, that no one wanders off alone and particularly that no one drowns!

Despite these concerns there exists some form of tranquility when you hear the excited screams of the kids having fun.

I was thankful to be swimming whenever I could during that summer and this particular time I didn't have Mark to look after so I took up a relaxing spot close to the shallow end of the pool and decided to keep a watch on the most populated region of the pool. Kids can turn anything into a game and I watched as a group of kids were inventing and creating their own fun, and was fascinated at how easy it was for kids to become friends and play together. As I was watching one particular game, which was a combination of 'Marco Polo' and ball toss (I won't even try to explain this one) I noticed a little boy in the midst of this game. He clearly wasn't playing the same game I was watching and he didn't even look as if he was a kid from the camp. He had blond hair, blue eyes and was content just paddling around. I noticed that his facial features resembled a rounded face, a face that I've seen on other children and adults but at the time didn't know that it was down syndrome; I had heard people using terms like 'Mongol' or 'Corky' (which at the time was a TV show played by someone that had identical facial features). I decided that I was going to just say 'Hi' to this kid. My hello was received well, and I found myself quickly in a game of tossing a ball between the two of us. I was having fun and so was my new friend. When we gave up the ball toss I gave a couple of pool launches, it's something that dad used to do to us when Andrew and I were kids and it always made us laugh and wanting more. So, I positioned myself and then launched my friend straight into the air, he would float through the air and then enter back into the water and I would wait to see his facial expression that tells you if someone wants another launch or not!

After a couple of launches I noticed a woman sitting on the deck with her feet in the pool looking at the two of us. Her face had a look that of a mother watching her son with a distinguished look of happiness and pride. I put two and two together and asked my new friend if that woman was his mother! Beside his mother was a young girl, who in my estimation had to have been her daughter and my new friend's sister. When he responded 'that is my mother and sister', my tactful ambush skills came to life. We connived a plan to get close to these women and then splash them with water!!! In all honesty they didn't see it coming; they were probably thinking that they were going to meet the guy that their family member had be-friended. So when the waves of water started to douse them, I could only imagine what they were thinking! It didn't last long, or rather; I was trying to be on better behavior after I splashed water on them and then was introduced to the boy that I had been playing with. His mother asked if he had introduced himself. Instantly I could tell that he was a bit shy, and introduced himself as 'Gregory'. 'Well it's nice to meet you, Gregory' I replied. I then met Greg's mom,

Jenny and sister Ashley. I had a brief conversation with them as the background noise indicated that the cattle were being herded up behind me and getting ready to head back to the campground. I mentioned that I was a camp councillor and starting my grade 11 year at Brother Andre Catholic High School in Markham. The engagement was short and there was no exchange of contact information or attempt to establish contact in the future. The encounter was pleasant and I never would have thought that such an innocent meeting would have a significant impact on my life to-date. There's a reason I noticed Greg in the pool that day and said 'hello', and as you will find out through the rest of this book it was not by accident, Greg and I were meant to meet and enable each other through friendship to reach levels we never would have imagined.

HIGH SCHOOL

Undoubtedly grade 11 was one of my most struggling years during high school. The sole reason for the challenges came through the teachers strike that year. Anyone who knows me also knows that during high school I was known for a couple of things. The most important thing would have been my sport involvement on the Brother Andre football and rugby teams. The other thing would have been my compassion for others, although that is what I perceive to have been my second important element that would have stood out in high school, some may have seen it differently.

The teacher strike really took a heartbeat out of my aspirations to play football that year. I was coming out of my grade 10 year holding both MVP (most valuable player) in both junior boys' football and in junior boy's rugby! I trained hard that summer to become a part of the varsity team in football at the start of school and play for a coach and person that I admired throughout high school, Mr. Terry Lyons. However, all those dreams came crashing down, when the Catholic school board union went on strike and the first thing that was cancelled were extracurricular activities, which meant for me, football.

Football kept my academic marks stable during the semester, without football that year I would go on to my second worst academic year in high school. The coaching staff posted a minimum of 65% average to stay eligible to play sports. When it became official that football was not going to happen, I barely stayed afloat with 60%. I was furious that football was cancelled that year; I was also young and spontaneous. I argued with teachers that hundreds of kids around the region would lose a valuable aspect of their social skills set with the loss of extracurricular activities. Teamwork, friendships, and the ability to learn ones' self, knowing ones' obstacles and finding ways to overcome those obstacles were cut out. I felt that sports and the clubs that existed after hours were more than just arenas for gatherings; they help to cultivate personalities, create bonds on playing fields and ice surfaces that would extend years beyond the classroom.

Being young and naïve about how union and systems worked at the time I took it upon myself to organize an entourage that would make a formal presentation to the Vice President of the Catholic School Board in Aurora, Ontario. I versed myself in a minimal understanding of the situation regarding the strike and the elements that teachers were struggling for. But at the end of the day, all I was concerned for were the students most of whom I never knew at the time were being deprived of this valuable aspect of life and growing up.

I held a few meetings with Mr. Lyons and a few other teachers that passed along words of encouragement to equip me for when I met with the board. I asked two other friends of mine to share in the presentation and at the time of the presentation power point hadn't taken off as mainstream in lectures and presentations so we composed notes and assigned different sections that we would each cover during the course of our interaction. Our biggest argument was that we found it unfair that adults could be so selfish and play in the world of politics on the backs of the students they chose as their vocational group to guide in life. My conversations with various teachers at the time brought back altering views on the situation. Most teachers expressed the desire to move on with the extra-curricular activities they were committed to, while others stood uncompromisingly on the side of the union. At the end of the day, there was no collective movement to re-instate sports and that is why I took it upon myself to find an avenue to try to save the Fall season. Mr. Lyons told me that if nothing were rectified by the first week of October, then the season would be lost for all groups that Fall and that put my efforts into overdrive.

It's comical looking back to that time, I cannot recall the classes that I was enrolled in that semester but I vividly recall the time and preparation I put into my big stand at the Catholic School Board Office, it's too bad that I didn't get marks assigned to my efforts with the strike, because I would have probably made honor roll that semester.

The weeks prior to my debut at the school board I organized a series of student lead protests. Please allow me to elaborate! I don't even know if my parents knew that I was the ringleader around the student protests that took place during my grade eleven year. When you hear the word protest it is easy to reflect on images of violence mixed with absurd action from those protesting and you may go as far as imagining a ringleader to be someone that is an instigator, a person whose ideals are stronger than anyone else's and to make a point they get their minions to do the dirty work they can't be seen doing!

Most protests can be violent or intrusive and counter-productive. I saw it a different way, you could say I saw things the way Mahatma Gandhi saw things when he lead his non-violence resistance. The last thing I wanted por-trayed was a school filled with youth that were insubor-dinate and intolerant of the situation. Gandhi wrote, "I object to violence because when it appears to do good, the good is only temporary, the evil it does is permanent"

(Mahatma Gandhi, Indian Political and spiritual leader, 1869 – 1948).

The last thing I wanted to happen was for any form of violence to occur; also I didn't want to be associated with a protest that would serve more harm than good. The idea that I had incorporated into effect was to hold a two-week uniform strike prior to the meeting scheduled at the school board. Since, Catholic Schools consistently wear a uniform it would be noticeable that the student population turn their uniforms in for their civilian clothing to make a statement, if I recall correctly the school would hold 'civi days' where students could wear their everyday clothing. The school mostly held a couple of 'civi days' each semester that would give students a break from the uniform. My version of non-resistance was holding a series of six 'civi days' in two weeks. I typed up a newsletter stating my concerns for my fellow students that were being deprived of their life beyond school, the injustice that was occurring and the experience they were missing out on. The newsletter wasn't overly long, and straight to the point. It clearly indicated the days that students were to NOT wear their uniforms and that if the collective mass didn't wear their uniform it would be expressed as a silent non-resistant protest. In addition, the newsletter indicated that this protest was only to include the not wearing of the uniform and that it was not a protest for students to further the issue to levels that would not be conducive for the purpose that I had intended it to be, especially as an excuse to skip out on class!!

After the printing of the newsletters I was ready to launch the student strike in an ad hoc way. A friend at a printing shop had printed the newsletters for free, which was excellent and kept my bank account untouched for this personal project. The following that I had gathered started to post newsletters around the school and started handing them out during the various lunch breaks in an attempt to reach everyone in the school. It was nerve racking, when everything started!!! By no means was I the most popular kid in the school, and worst was that I couldn't predict the outcome of my perceived goal. I didn't do an overly detailed job of surveying a majority of students to get their thoughts and opinions on the strike and went from the standpoint that most students felt just like I did!

There must have been hundreds of newsletters printed and handed out within a day. The school staff knew what was going on, but fortunately for me all newsletters were handed out and the ship had already left the harbor. The first day of wearing 'civies' came faster than I expected and I was by no means disappointed! Students from all grades were in their everyday clothes and hung up their uniforms. Classes continued which was what I was hoping for, and the students that wore their uniform were the minority, and would go on to not wear their uniforms on the remaining days of the 'student strike'.

Mom and Dad always taught me to never boast about your position, and that it was better if someone else boasted about you! So when I was called into the Vice Principal's office and asked if I was the initiator of the 'strike' in progress I admitted to the omission. The VP surprisingly did not give me a hard time, nor did he threaten with suspension or detention. It took a while for the staff to find me as the culprit and when they did, the only question that was asked that day in the VP's office was, "Why did you not put your name on the newsletters that were circulated and take ownership for your actions?" How interesting that his concern was not why I did what I did but why my name was absent on the newsletters. My answer was simple, "Sir, by no means did I want to be singled out as the instigator of this collective action, I didn't feel the need to have my name on the newsletter, because then it would give the impression to students that they should follow my ideologies. I wanted each student that cared about the injustice that was occurring to make that choice on their own, and not because Dan Rossi came up with this idea. I am not ashamed of what I have done, and I would readily admit to anyone who asks of my involvement in this matter". It goes with what I was taught about not boasting about myself.

Day 5 of the movement brought two noteworthy elements to my cause. The first was that various news crews had heard about what we were doing and came to the school to capture what was going on. Local papers came with cameras primed and ready to expose our collective action – 'our collective action'!!! So when I wasn't summoned by any news group or reporters to be in any pictures or footage or even mentioned by the people that were claiming to take the responsibility for the student strike, I was not upset in the slightest! Nothing was pointing to me, and that is exactly what I wanted, I didn't want any kind of hero status for something that was on the majority of student's minds at my school and across the region. I simply wanted to create a venue for others to demonstrate their concern for their loss of school afterlife.

The second thing that happened on Day 5 of the strike would be more memorable to me than anything else I would have done in high school. That was also the day that I met Ashley O'Brien, Greg's sister. Ashley had found me at my locker and approached me, and for the life of me I couldn't place her to my memory until she disclosed that she was the sister of the friend that I had met in the pool at summer's past. Of course I remembered the blond hair, blue eye'd Down syndrome boy, and I could slightly recall the two women sitting on the pool's edge that were the victims of Greg's and my splashing. Ashley had a question for me from her mother. Her mother was wondering if I would be a friend to her son and hang out with him and if I would call her to give her my answer or any questions that I may have had. God will put things right in front of you sometimes and I was ready and willing to accept this request. Nervous and uncertain it didn't matter because my answer was yes!

Day 6 of the strike was uneventful, in the sense that it was the last unplanned 'civi' day and the final post before I approached the school board with my youthful zest. The meeting with the Vice President of the Catholic School Board was scheduled in the afternoon on a Monday, I had no problem skipping my afternoon classes to meet with the lady that I thought could swing her gavel and put an end to the strike so I could play football and other students could participate in their own after school interests. I was convinced and so were my co-presenters that we were going to leave her office with a victory. Looking back I was very optimistic and I remained optimistic to the day, however, I was in for a shock that day at the school board.

My team was given the floor first, and with passion and charisma we stated our concern and expectations for the course of action to precede our meeting, which was to have teachers available to run their respective after school activities and restore all sport teams for that fall semester. The rebuttal in my opinion failed miserably. Her first words were, "When I was in high school, I was on the girl's volleyball team and loved the friendships, bonds and experience that came along with the sport....BUT". It's easy to stereotype people at times, and when the vice-president started to engage us my optimism disappeared, and I immediately stereotyped her for her opening sentence. Everyone knows that when they hear that word 'but' there is nothing good that follows, you know that you've already lost the battle of opinions when the opposing party uses 'but'. What they are saying is that, 'sure, I see your point, and I agree with you, BUT, I don't see it that way, therefore, we will keep things the way they are and thanks for coming out'.

How many international delegations are held up because the first words out of world leaders is the word 'but'? It's a tragedy to resort to that word in most conversations, because it has stalled peace talks, prolonged domestic arguments, and built walls between people around the world.

Walking away from that meeting I knew that we had lost our case, the union was adamant they cease all after school activities until a resolution came into effect that was pleasing to them and I could only imagine how many times they used the word 'but' at their negotiation table. Despite losing my football season, I had another door open to me and that door would turn into the gateway for a friendship that I will try to explain to you throughout the remaining pages of this book.

IT WAS A JOB

I took Ashley and her mother up on their offer and made the phone call to see what exactly I was getting myself involved with. Jenny O'Brien was pleasant on the phone, and her offer was pretty sweet. In a nutshell, she was asking that I be a friend with Greg, take him out once or twice a week, play sports here and there and for my efforts I would get $20 bucks! Not a bad deal, I was sixteen years old, at the time I was working at the local grocery store the 'Garden Basket' and thought that $20.00 extra dollars wasn't a bad thing on top of what I was bringing home. I was excited, I told Mom about the new venture I was diving into. I decided that for our first outing I would take Greg to Markville Mall which happened to be down the street from where he lived. I showed up to the O'Brien's house with the kind of excitement you get when you start a new job or before you set foot on the rugby pitch or football field. How do you prepare to become someone's friend? I felt as though it was some kind of blind date set-up, Greg was my junior by five years and I will attest to feeling a bit awkward the first day. No matter how outgoing I could be I still felt the discomfort of meeting someone new to me. When I stepped into the O'Brien residence I felt the same way I did when I stepped into John's house two years prior, shy, quiet and doubting my ability. I quickly noticed Jenny's motherly touch with her son. I remember Jenny having this loving look on her face and a brightness that gave her this 'alive' look. Looking back, that's all I remember from meeting Jenny...she took a chance with me, I don't have children of my own but know that trusting a stranger with the care of your children can be extremely difficult. Without being facetious Jenny made a good choice.

Greg was excited to go to the mall after I told him my plans for the afternoon. The mall was our first outing, we both piled into my 1995 Blue Ford pick-up truck which I called "Frank the Tank", introduced Greg to my wheels and how I referred to my truck by the name I gave it and talked about my truck as though he were a person and not an object. Greg liked the fact that I had a truck named 'Frank' and Frank was going to take us to the mall (on a side note I still give names to the cars I drive, and I can't foresee that changing anytime soon!). On the way to the mall, Greg was telling me how much he loved Britney Spears, and asked me if I had a CD of hers. I knew who the singer was, heck, Britney and I were around the same age but I had to admit that I wasn't really into her music much. Rest assured Greg had a CD of the pop star icon, and that would be my first introduction to the love that Greg had for music.

When we arrived, the mall was packed; malls tend to be a gathering ground for students of the surrounding schools in the area. Markville Mall has a notable food court entrance that at the time used to be right beside a Cineplex Odeon. When you walk in, there is an overwhelming scent of fried food, and ambient noise from those gathered around the numerous tables surrounding the food court. I never thought to ask Greg if he felt like something to drink or eat, I mean what else do you do at a mall? I've never been one for shopping and really the only time I was in the mall was to eat! I had the wonderful plan of going to the mall, but once we got there I had no idea of what to do! I completely dislike malls, and I was baffled as to why I would bring Greg there when I myself thought it to be an empty idea. As we maneuvered through the crowd I thought that Greg would like to go to the Toys 'R' Us as a starter. I have to admit that even though I may not like malls, how could you not like Toys 'R' Us!

Andrew and I didn't have too many toys when we were kids, but we had plenty of 'Lego'. That's where we started, the Lego section, I still stand in amazement of the new ideas that Lego comes out with, although it has been years since I've assembled any kind of masterpiece, I relish in the fact that the company keeps coming out with fantastic new ideas every year. Unfortunately for me, Greg wasn't really into Lego like I was, the stuffed animals were kind of a hit but what really topped the cake were the 'WWF' figurines. My 'Nonno' (Italian for grandfather) loved WWF wrestling. Nonno actually brought me to a WWF match at the old Maple Leaf Gardens; we sat in the nose bleed section, but still could see the massiveness of the wrestlers as they entered the ring. I had never seen men so large in my life and when 'Andre the Giant' entered the stadium his grandness was felt by everyone! Andre had this one-piece black suit trademark with a single strap over one of his shoulders. The only other wrestler that I knew was the infamous 'Hulk Hogan', known for the ripping of his yellow tank top before he entered the ring, stomped to and fro in the ring, jumped on the turnbuckles and brought one hand to his ear invoking the crowd to give their unfailing cheerful response. That was about it, Nonno would watch wrestling almost every time it was on TV, but I thought it was a tad farfetched and didn't really get into it. Greg on the other hand shared a different view; he could name all the wrestling figurines that were on the shelf that day at Toys 'R' Us. Not only that, Greg was playing with the figu-rines for at least half an hour as well. I joined Greg with the matches that he set up between the different characters and made sound effects to correspond with the brutal-ity of getting beaten up. I felt my time was coming to an end with the wrestlers so I suggested to Greg that we go somewhere else in the mall for a bit and do something different. Well, that was easier said than done, Greg was up for doing something else, but he posted a condition that the only way he was leaving Toys 'R' Us was with me buying him a wrestling figurine! At first I thought it was a bit cute, 'sure I'll buy you a figurine...for Christmas'! I told Greg. Oh, believe me that did not cut it for Greg one bit; Greg started a routine that I had never been exposed to before. I probably did it to my parents but I never would have thought in my wildest dreams that I would be a victim of the 'whine', when a child wants something! Oh, boy, did Greg put up a fuss, he was adamant that I buy the Hulk Hogan for him and that if we were friends I would do it happily. This was our first outing, how the heck was I going to handle this situation? I was stumped, I didn't even have a cell phone to call Jenny to seek advice, it was just Greg, Hulk Hogan and me! That started the creative input to get Greg out of the store without giving in to his demands. I faintly remembered Jenny telling me not to buy him anything, and if I had any sense I should have asked, 'well, what do I do if he wants me to buy him something'? I was stuck; I threw out all my options, 'I don't have money', 'how about I buy you this for your birthday or Christmas'? Nothing was working; I even pretended speaking to the store manager on a nearby store phone attached to a pillar, suggesting that it wasn't a good idea to buy the toy at this time! At my wits end, I pulled out the ultimate last resort...the walk away! Oh, I felt horrible; I walked around the corner, acted like I was walking out, and then waited! To my surprise there was no effect, Greg just sat there playing away, 10 minutes must have passed before Greg took serious notice that I had disappeared. He put down the toy, stood up, and started leisurely walking towards the front of the store. I scurried in front of him because I didn't want Greg to catch me in the store so I practically ran out, caught my breath and waited. Greg emerged from the store and didn't seem to mind that he left without Hulk Hogan. I made a mental note to never take Greg to Toys 'R' Us ever again!

If I knew at the time what I know now, I wouldn't have taken Greg to the next stop during our first encounter either! HMV! Greg loves music, absolutely loves music and, at the time when he mentioned that he liked Brittany Spears I was hoping to go and listen to some of her songs from her first CD. All I knew of her was 'Hit Me Baby One More Time' song and the music video when she was wearing a short school uniform skirt that made her famous with the guys my age not to mention the guys older than me at the time.

There definitely was a Brittany buzz at HMV, there were loads of advertising for her 'Day-bout' CD, and they even had a poster size cardboard print of her in that school uniform. It didn't take long for Greg to find the Brittany section. I gawked at the price of a CD; I thought it was way over priced at over $20.00! Greg seemed quite content sitting in front of the Brittany section reading the back of the CD.

At the time I met Greg I was in my third year of ballroom and Latin dance lessons with mom! Music was a big part of my life, but I rarely bought a CD, and I have never downloaded any songs. I would rather save the money I would spend on a CD for something that I would be able to use practically! So I perused about the store, which didn't last very long before I felt the need to move on yet again. After coming out of Toys 'R' Us you would think I would have anticipated what was going to happen next...'Dan, I want you to buy me this CD', is what Greg said as I approached where he was sitting! Here we go again", was my response.

What had I done to be put through this? I looked at the price of the CD again, added up the tax and it was well over the $20.00 dollars that Jenny was going to pay me, and told Greg that it wasn't going to happen! I quickly deployed all my tactics that I found in the previous store, I even left twice this time and nothing!!! I was shocked; it was like the last stand of the 'OK Corral' from Wyatt Earp! Neither of us were giving in and the end was nowhere in sight. At this point Greg had gathered a crowd, after the second time I left and returned I found two girls that were working at HMV crouched down beside him asking him what was wrong. Like M&M's in your mouth these girls just melted! Greg gave them such a story of how I wouldn't buy him this gift and that's all he wanted. The girls immediately took his side; confidently they turned to me and asked, "Why don't you just buy him the CD?" Yeah, right I thought, you have no idea what I've been through and all you can do is suggest to me to give in and buy this CD, and I don't even particularly like Brittany Spears!

It was day one with Greg and I didn't want him thinking that friends would buy anything that their friends requested. It doesn't happen that way, and I didn't want to put our relationship in danger from the get go if I simply bought everything that Greg was asking from me that day. I figured that if I was going to be friends with Greg he needed to respect the fact that friendship went beyond 'buying' things for each other.

The girls at the store started getting on my nerves, and I had to hold my tongue from saying things that probably wouldn't have been role model material. Greg put on such a good show that they gave in, and handed Greg a free issue of a 'Backstreet Boys' CD and another CD from an unknown artist to him! Boom, matter settled, Greg got what he wanted and I started to like this kid.

It makes me laugh when I think about how that day played out! Greg won the battle but he didn't win the war! At the end of our excursion, I was paid the $20.00 dollars and had a chuckle about my first experience with Greg!

Our future outings took a different look, and trust me there were no more mall trips planned. Since football was out, I took Greg to our field one afternoon and planned on passing the ball. I had a bit of a gift for Greg that day and it was my last season's football jersey. My number was 31, which was what Mike 'Pinball' Clemons wore for his time with the Toronto Argonauts. This was something that I had done with John so when he came to my games he would have my previous year's jersey to wear and it was also a way for me to help John feel as though he was very much a part of the team. I showed up with the jersey and told Greg that when football started the next year I wanted him to wear the jersey with pride and know that he would be on the field just as much as I was. Greg and I started tossing the ball back and forth, and then it happened... Greg wanted to be on the same team and play against an imaginary defense. Greg started out as the quarterback, and would toss a 5-10 yard pass to me, in which I would run and pretend to be tackled by some mammoth linebacker hunting me down. Once we would get into scoring range Greg would ask for the ball, either a handoff or a quick pass and he would sprint it into the end zone! Now when Greg sprints there is nothing quite like it, to say the least it's endearing, it's not overly fast but you know that Greg is running with all his might. It was a tough game, and when Greg was tackled he would gracefully fall, do a quick roll and get up ready to do it again. It reminded me of my time with John and the basketball games against Michael Jordan and Scottie Pippen! I was having fun, I had done this before, making myself vulnerable and playing as though Greg and I were in front of thousands of fans cheering us on! It was in that moment that I questioned what I was doing. I was hanging out with a kid that had a disability in the eyes of society and yet, I was starting to feel through our outings that we were becoming friends. Until that point, my time with Greg was due to his mother asking me to help her out and I would get paid for it, it was just another job and it was at that moment I realized that I couldn't do it anymore. I told myself that I couldn't keep hanging out with Greg if I accepted money for being his friend, because friends don't do that. I have never paid anyone to hang out with me nor have I had anyone pay me to hang out with them and yet, I was being paid to hang out with Greg. Jenny was good enough to send money for when we had an ice cream or drink, but I looked at the $20.00 dollars she was paying me as revenue, and it was then that I realized I was making a fatal error in our friendship. It was a revelation and from that moment on, I knew that if Greg and I were to continue being friends I would not accept money to hang out with him.

We packed up our equipment we brought to the field, Greg had my old jersey and we jumped into Frank to take us back to Greg's place. On the ride home Frank was bumping with Brittany Spears through his stereo system. From the field we had been playing in to Greg's house there were only a handful of lights and we got every red light on the way which really didn't matter because there was a dance floor inside of Frank that turned more than a couple of heads. Remember, Brittany Spears wasn't really my thing, but that day she finally took my ear and I was jamming, even though I would joke with Greg and tell him that Brittany and I were dating, it was really only ever my ear that she took. Now generally when a good song goes through Frank, and I like it, there is a bunch of moves that I bust out. Dancing with Greg at red lights blaring Brittany Spears was no different that day! Greg has this thing where he would roll down the window and sing as loudly as he can out the window and as you can imagine, this definitely drew the attention of those sharing the road with us. For the most part people were smiling as we rocked out, I could see smiles, which told me that people received it well and that they either thought it was cute or silly – it doesn't really matter because we weren't stopping ☺.

As we rolled into Greg's driveway I'm sure that the neighbors could hear what we were listening to. After each visit, when we entered the O'Brien's residence, I would stand in the front foyer and update Jenny on what had transpired through our outing. I would tell her the good and the bad, and admit to some of the goofy stuff that we did and only wonder what she would think of me when I told her! After the debrief I would usually get money for my time. But that day it was different, on that day, I realized that over the months that had passed Greg and I had legitimately become friends and I couldn't take the money. Jenny insisted but, my heart had already been altered and a friendship secured. When I drove home that day I was shocked at myself, I could not believe that I had been accepting money to hang out with someone that truly had impacted my life and I could call a friend.

From that day on, Jenny continued sending Greg with money so he could learn the responsibility of paying for things himself and on the other hand to ensure that I wasn't paying for everything.

GRADE 11 COMING TO AN END

The remainder of grade 11 went like this.... I started volunteering at the local hospital because I watched the movie called 'Patch Adams' and wanted to experience what it was like to work in a hospital. I was enrolled in a program at school called 'Community Arts which was an integrated program for students with disabilities that were matched up with another student and enjoyed a friendship throughout the semester. The program was guided towards a mutual engagement of vulnerability and adaptability. On my side I had to learn different techniques to engage people with disabilities and how to use multiple communication skills to both pass and receive information. In addition, it was benefiting watching fellow students in my position develop their cross-communication skills and take what I liked about their individual approaches and decide for myself the tactics that worked well and the tactics that did not work as well. Another benefit was that at the time of enrollment, unbeknownst to me, I was the only male student in the class but always a nice surrounding for a high school kid.

CHAPTER EIGHT

GREG JUST ASKED FOR ONE TOUCHDOWN

Your friend is your needs answered.

- Kahlil Giban

*Greg in the orange his friend in yellow and me giving
them a hug after Christmas tree chopping!!!*

*Our first performance on Television at the Rogers Studio
in York Region. From Left to Right:
Andrew Rossi – Marcel Destine, Greg O'Brien, Daniel
Rossi and Miles Krauter.*

*Greg and I in our version of a firefighters calendar – a gift
that Greg put together for his family (2001).*

*Greg and the Boys first performance at our
graduating high school – Brother Andre.*

A photo from one of our practices – the laughter is indicative of how much fun we would have when we got together!!!!

Andrew and Miles practicing 'Larger Than Life" by the Backstreet Boys.

*Greg and the Boys performing at Tim Horton's Camp
Day, June 2009.*

Practice - Practice and more Practice.

*Greg and The Boys at a photo-shoot before our Concert at
the University of Guelph in February 2006.*

*Greg never really enjoyed dancing!!! So, Andrew, Rob
and I knew how to throw it down at any given time.*

Greg and The Boys at our Concert at the Richmond Hill Theater April 1ˢᵗ, 2010.

Greg's favorite spot to hang out – Tim Horton's – drinking his most beloved drink of all time - The Ice Cappuccino !!!!!!!!

Greg and the Boys second television performance before our concert at the Markham Theater on May 2nd 2009.

It was the first bowl game of the year for my football team; last year's strike resulted in our junior boy's football team being amalgamated with our senior team, which resulted in one varsity team for the school. There were only seven senior players on the team – meaning there were a total of seven players in grade 12 and up and the rest of the team were in junior high. This was the year that I got to play for my high school mentor and coach, Terry Lyons, who announced that it would be his last year of coaching at Brother Andre CHS, as he would be moving to Windsor to pursue a principal position with a school there. This meant that I had one opportunity to impress Mr. Lyons one last time on the field.

In football, the reputation that I held, in my opinion, was interesting. I wouldn't say that I was the best player on the team, arguable, but at least I never thought of myself as the best player, however, what I would pride myself with, was the determination and hard work ethic I brought to the field, to practice and to off-season training which could have been second to none. Because I wasn't the best, did not mean that I wasn't talented, I was up there with the best of players on the team but set aside because of my attitude and leadership skills.

The challenger to our first bowl game that year was Father Bressani Catholic High School playing us in the Catholic bowl and since they were the only other catholic high school at the time that had a team, they were the only team that could challenge us in the match. Father Bressani was known throughout the league as being 'behind the play, players', all that meant was whenever they could take a cheap shot at a player they would.

High school football pre-game was something of a spectacle, players would wear their uniform to school that day, which automatically set them apart from the rest of the school population – some would skip class...some would go to all their classes. Our change room was a small gymnasium 70 feet away from the field and there were no benches, just an open gym. Some players would listen to music through CD players, some would change in the same spot every time, and others would just change in quiet as they mentally prepared for the game. I can't really say that I had any particular pre-game strategy. But that year I was conscious about the fact that all the senior players on the team were looking forward to playing for Mr. Lyons, and voluntarily forfeited my position as captain for one of the OAC players on the team to lead us out of the dressing room or to go for the coin toss on my behalf. I thought that I had another year of football after this one, so I was content with sharing the experience of being in front of the team.

Football is magical; there are very few experiences that can match up to the excitement of being a football player. The suiting up of your equipment holds the same chivalrous honor as a knight putting on his armor in preparation for battle. Players were like soldiers of old; all had their own responsibilities while at the same time looking out for each other, sharing the battlefield that inevitably would hold one team as victorious over the other.

Our team tradition was unique to us, the captains would lead the team onto the field where we would run a lap or two for warm up, form 4 lines in front of each of the captains and start a stretch routine. At the end of our warm up we would sound off on 20 jumping jacks as loud as we could to let the other team know that we were here and ready for action. The coin toss called upon each team's captain, that year I was the offensive captain, and although I played on the other side of the ball, my primary duty was to the offensive. Each team had four captains, I don't really know where that practice came from but I know that not everyone has had the experience of being called up to take the coin toss and stand directly in front of your opponent, see their eyes behind the protective cage and try to act with an aura of intimidation and confidence. I found it rather humorous at times as the level of seriousness at these coin tosses was a tad extreme and although I would portray seriousness and confidence I couldn't help but smile as these titans held themselves in an almost unnatural behavior.

While the captains were at the coin-toss ceremony, the rest of the team would form a horseshoe and a combination of two hand slaps to the thigh pads, followed by one clap with the hands in the famous beat brought to us by "Queen", 'We will rock you' as choreographed by one of the players, would take place. As the toss started to come to an end the beat would quicken up in anticipation for the captains to come running through the middle of the horseshoe then become surrounded by the rest of the team jumping up and down for a bit and then...'ONE, TWO, THREE – CARDINALS' as loud as possible. When I was a captain, I didn't particularly like being jumped on by my fellow teammates in the middle of elevated testosterone equipment wearing football players. When I went up for the coin-toss I would gather the three other captains, say a prayer for protection and safety before we ran into the chaos.

That game I allowed my fullback, who was an OAC student, to take the coin toss in my place and for the first time since Grade Nine I was on the outskirts of the 'horseshoe' ceremony and I took my place at one end of the horseshoe, falling in line, playing the beat. For me it was interesting to see who the other leaders of the team were as some would call the cadence while others would yell words to get others fired up! I remember the four captains running towards the opening of the horseshoe, knowing how it would collapse on them before the final countdown was initiated. I remember liking the outside position. Everyone had less than a millimeter between them and I was quite comfortable being an arm's length away from the excitement. My excitement came from the quiet confidence of knowing what I had to do and more importantly knowing that I could do it. I was set apart on the team for doing one thing that no one else had ever done.

My high school football 'career' started with John standing on the sidelines at our home games wearing my previous year's jersey right beside our team and now this year Greg dawned my previous year's jersey number 31 and looked like he was wearing a dress in comparison. I hardly left the field, playing both offence and defense but when I could, either on a time out or a change I would run by and give Greg a quick hi. Greg was such a good fan, Greg has a voice that is quite distinct when he yells, you can hear him a mile away. Greg will throw out a combination of encouraging words and threaten those that would tackle me, which was more often than not as I was the running back. Greg totally understood the game of football and only had one wish when he watched me play, and that was to get a 'touchdown'. I would always chuckle when he would state his expectations and my default was, 'Greg I'll do my best but I don't always get a touchdown'. I didn't want to make a promise I couldn't keep but relished in the opportunity to give Greg his wish.

The game was close, a lot closer than it should have been, our lead heading into the fourth quarter was only by one touchdown and error for margin was slim. Father Bressani was kicking the ball on fourth down and I was set up 40 yards away waiting to return the kick. As you stand behind 23 players, there's a certain quiet, the night was chilly and under the spotlights I could see the cold exhaust leaving the players mouths like idling cars. I could see Greg on the sideline and decided that when I caught the ball I would run towards the sideline that Greg was on.

As the ball was kicked, I followed it through the air, never taking my mind off of it, knowing full well that there were 12 players running full steam to stop my attempt of a return and in that moment you feel scared and excited at the same time. When you catch that ball, and bring your eyes to the field you have less than a second to make a decision as to where you'll run and where the open field lurks. I had a pre-determined plan to run on the sideline to my left where Greg was, most times returns are more ad hoc than anything because you can't rely on a pre-determined path to run because it is all variable on the players pursuing you and you merely adapt to their positioning. As I made the catch I headed straight towards the sideline, tucking the ball into my arm, trying to get to the outside of the pursing players before they got the angle on me that would stop my momentum and I ran. As I passed my team on the sidelines I could hear the cheers of excitement as all I had was an open field ahead of me, and then there was Greg, head down and talking to a girl! I ran into the end-zone and was followed by my team mates that celebrated more than I did when I scored. I made an attempt to hand the referee the ball after a touchdown in a gesture of good faith. I ran from the cluster in the end-zone towards Greg, as I approached I asked "Hey, did you see that?" Greg was all too honest and said "What, did you score?" Oh, I could have tackled him myself, it wasn't as if I scored all the time and he didn't even see it. I just rolled my eyes and chuckled it off saying "well make sure you watch the next one will ya", as I trotted off. That was my first ever kick return touchdown and when I rejoined the team panting, there was a flag on the ground and a penalty against my team, which meant that all my effort, all that running and eluding, the touchdown didn't even count. We were called for holding and I couldn't believe that it was all for none. Father Bressani decided to kick again, and Mr. Lyons wanted to switch me up for a relief since I had just sprinted 60 or so yards. I told him that I was fine and would go back in.

I took my spot at the same distance and don't think that I had a pre-determined plan the second time, and what were the chances of returning for a second score? As the ball soared through the air, I followed its arc until it landed in my arms. My quick assessment of the situation, made me cut right as my first step to elude an opponent. I started to run to the right side of the field, which was on the opposite side of the field that my team was on. I eluded another opponent who prompted me to change my direction left at this point, a couple of blocks and I found myself with some running room. I started to build up some speed, took off to the sideline and was being pursued by Father Bressani's kicker who was their last line of defense. The cheering started all over again, it doesn't happen often that you get to run past your team, ball in hand while heading for the end-zone! That game I had it twice in back-to-back plays. I outran the defender and was barraged by an even bigger parade of excited team-mates. But the best part was that Greg saw the whole thing this time!

I was knackered this time round, after I got up from the pile that amassed on top of me, I trotted towards Greg – who had a grin on his face from ear to ear. He had seen it and more importantly I came through with what he wanted from me and Greg was celebrating as if he was the one who scored! That moment was more memorable to me than when I celebrated with my teammates. It was special to me because I knew that Greg wasn't able to play football and I knew that he had the heart to, the excitement to, but wouldn't be able to play at the level I could for obvious reasons and it meant a lot to me to have Greg be a part of a team and experience that I cherished. It's important that I share this story, you see on the surface it appears as a re-telling of my short-lived football career, self-indulgence, however, it is more than that. When Greg would ask me to score him a touchdown he did something to me, he allowed me to become more attentive to what others valued. Greg would go on telling me certain things that he wanted in life, and as our friendship grew so would my ability to make the things that he asked for come true or at least the dreams he would share with me. The world would rotate a thousand times over when I was able to be a part of one of Greg's many dreams, dreams that you will read about and dreams that still wait patiently for us both.

WHAT IS DOWN SYNDROME?

You have probably seen people who have Down syndrome or something referred to as 'Downs'. They have certain physical features such as a flatter face and upward slanting eyes. They have more medical problems than the rest of us such as more susceptibility to heart defects, and diabetes. Kids with Down Syndrome usually have trouble learning and are slower to learn how to talk and take care of themselves with larger than normal tongues communication can be a great hindrance. But despite their challenges, kids with Down Syndrome can go to regular schools, make friends, enjoy life and get jobs when they're older. Getting special help early – often when they are just babies and toddlers – can be the key to healthier, happier and more independent lives. In my experience, this is the biggest key to a better quality of life for those living with Downs or exceptionalities. I've met many parents of children with disabilities, good examples to bad examples, and I've tried not to judge, but can't say I have not, as it would be a lie. Despite, what I've seen, I know that a loving and caring family is the biggest element to any child's success in this world, especially a child with a disability. If you can recall, Mark's sister was extremely compassionate towards her brother, loving and constantly positive. I have known Greg for 12 years now, and subsequently I have known his parents and his sister for the same duration. What I have seen in that household, the love towards Greg, the support, the patience and compassion is award winning. If such an award could be given for love, I would want to co-present that award with a notable leader in our country.

Some of the greatest compliments that I have received on Greg's behalf are that some of my friends didn't know that Greg had a disability – now that hasn't happened often but it has happened. That is a testament to Greg's upbringing! Most children with Down syndrome are very difficult to understand and as I mentioned, having larger than usual tongues you and I would struggle trying to decipher what they were trying to convey. Some children have uncontrollable behavior problems or social issues, and the list goes on. Yet, Greg is not the norm, he's Down syndrome through and through but his parents have invested so much time with Greg through speech therapy and integration that you might not think there was anything wrong with Greg at all. I will explain a bit later, however, often times there is no way of knowing that a child will be born with a disability – perhaps more so as scientist play with genetic selection and gene manipulation, however, when a child is born to parents and they enter this world with a disability I could not imagine how they take the news in that moment when they find out that their son or daughter has a disability. It must be hard, it must be frustrating and they must feel a sense of loss or blame. Parents with children born with disabilities have one of the highest divorce rates and as if it is not difficult enough to raise a child with a disability, imagine having to do it on your own. The task would be insurmountable and yet there are parents out there doing just that.

WITH DOWN SYNDROME CHROMOSOMES ARE THE CAUSES:

To understand why Down syndrome happens, you need to understand a little about chromosomes. What are chromosomes? They are thread-like structures within each cell and made up of genes. Genes provide the information that determines everything about people, from hair color to whether they are girls or boys. Most people have 23 pairs of chromosomes, for a total of 46. But a baby with Down Syndrome has an extra chromosome (47) instead of (46) or one chromosome has an extra part. This extra genetic material causes problems with the way their bodies develop.

DO A LOT OF PEOPLE HAVE DOWN SYNDROME?

You might already know that we get our chromosomes from our mother and father and half of those are from your mother and the other half from your father. You may think that there is something wrong with the parent which is not the case. The truth is that doctors don't know why this chromosome problem happens, however, about 1 out of every 800 babies born has Down Syndrome, no matter what race or nationality the parents are. No one gets

Down Syndrome later in life and it is not contagious so you can't catch it from someone else. You are born with it.

It is very easy to look at a child with a disability and feel sorry for them or for their parents, however, I believe that God has made each of us in a very unexplainable beautiful pattern regardless of race or disability. There is the beauty about each of us that is worth telling a story about. I wouldn't be writing a story about a boy with Down Syndrome who had such a big impact on my life if it wasn't true. I never thought that Greg understood the value of friendship or the meaning of love until he proved me wrong. I was ignorant to the fact that we are made in God's image and have a destination in life that will lead us to influence the life of another. When Greg proved me wrong, I changed my ideology to what I've just shared with you. Some of the biggest lessons that I have learned in life have not come from the professors that I've listened to in lecture nor the great leaders of our time trying to rid the world of poverty or aids. No, the most valuable lessons that I've learned have come from a boy with Down Syndrome that could easily be passed up because of what he looks like or the label he carries. I can say with my head held high with pride, that Greg allowed me to become his friend and began this learning process for me.

CHAPTER NINE

HIGH SCHOOL FOR GREG AND I

'Daniel, I don't care what we do all I want is an ICE CAP'!

- Greg O'Brien

When I entered my last year of high school, Greg was entering his first year and we would share a full year at the same school before I would graduate! The summer prior, I enjoyed some good times with Greg. That was the summer that Tim Horton's came out with a drink that would capture Greg's taste buds to this day – the famous 'ICE CAP'. I firmly believe that with the amount of money Greg has spent on ice caps since the summer of 2001 when they were first introduced, he could have used it to buy his own Tim Horton's. The man loves his ice cap and guess what his biggest gifts are to him for birthday or Christmas – you guessed it, Tim Horton gift certificates! That was also the summer that I finally broke down and admitted to enjoying the music by Brittany Spears and the Backstreet Boys.

At this point in my life, I was a member of the Canadian Armed Forces Reserve and spent three quarters of the summer away at basic recruit training and felt a new sense of worth for having gone through the process of joining the military and joining the ranks of such an honorable organization.

When September rolled around I was excited for the new football season. The previous year the team failed to reach the playoffs and with a year of playing together under our belt I felt confident that we would have the talent to be contenders. As a senior, what better dream to have than to walk away from one's last year winning the region's top spot as the best football team.

That year God had a different plan, one that was not easy for me to understand at first but would come to understand with time.

Football practices were different that year, Terry Lyons had moved on and we still had a varsity team, which meant that we had all grades represented on the team. Nonetheless, I was excited, when our first exhibition game came along, our team was looking good, we defeated our opponent by 3 scores and I was able to run in for two of them! With one game before our season opener, the coaches usually ran us through our special team plays. They are not the most practiced but it's a good cool down, low-pressure practice before games. Last year's performance of two punt returns in a row landed me a spot on the return squad for a second year. I admittedly enjoyed the return position, I liked the quiet before the storm, it never ceased to amaze me – when the ball was soaring through the air that was all you saw and heard, then when you caught it the world came rushing back into action and you had to rely on your quick feet and quick decision-making skills. Practice was no different for me; I still had the same experience returning kicks, except this time there came a little twist. As I was behind the team awaiting the kick, I began my assessment of the configuration of the offence prior to the kick, how many guys did they have wide, who was likely to be the first down the field and what direction would I go to? Although these were all my teammates, I still would approach practices like they were games. The kick was up in the air, I knew the kicker and I knew that he could put some weight behind the kick so I thought 50 yards was generous. As I followed the ball through the air, I self corrected as the arc on the ball was high rather than far so I raced to meet the ball's trajectory as it re-entered the atmosphere. I caught it with ease but noticed that almost immediately there was a defender almost right on top of me, I quickly faked right, then pushed off left trying to elude the defender when I felt a pain like never before. I didn't know what it was but I knew it wasn't good, I knew that in the step off I tore something in my knee that brought me straight to the ground screaming and clutching my right knee. All sense of movement ceased, the team surrounded me, which made me feel most uncomfortable. The guy I tried to elude was apologizing, coaches were asking for room, I saw cleats, I felt pain, I knew that I was done, and at that moment I knew that I wouldn't be able to play that year. Practice was done after that, I managed to hobble to the sideline and one of the statistic girls brought me an ice pack and sympathetically told me that everything would be all right and that I was going to bounce back. I had to hold back the tears because I knew my body better than anyone and it was telling me something different. The team was somber. Andrew had to drive home that night as I couldn't bend my knee and he too was quiet. Andrew played on the defense and was in grade 11 at the time, he too felt the injury as did the rest of the team. All my excitement for the season was gone, my drive, my hard work my desire to win and lead the team to victory was gone and I felt lost.

The doctor confirmed that I had torn my Anterior Cruciate Ligament (ACL) and that I wouldn't be able to play the season and with surgery booked on my birthday in February of that year I would be in recovery during the rugby season, so his advice for me was to find another hobby.

It was one of the most difficult times for me, my goals and aspirations in high school were sports. I would wake up and watch TSN for the previous night's highlights and sport stories – I was devastated! As a result of my injury I stepped down as the team captain, I stopped attending practices and missed out on the first couple of games as well. Unknown to me at the time, my teammates had all added my player #7 onto their jerseys and when I heard of this it brought tears to my eyes. I was touched to realize that I was so highly thought of yet sad that I couldn't join my friends and teammates on the field for our last year together.

The first game that I dragged my feet to was the bowl game against Father Bressani. Just like the previous year it was under the night-lights of our home field and a significant crowd base came out to watch. My cane gave me away as being injured, and my jersey over a pair of jeans replaced the padded equipment and tights as my dress. On the right shoulder sleeves of my teammate's jerseys you could clearly see a white number seven on their red colored jerseys. I went to the game with Greg that year and as I stood on the sideline I couldn't help but recall the success that our team accomplished the year prior. Greg was beside me the whole game, wearing my number 31; the holes on the shoulders were battle scares of my grade 10 year as a running back. My new jersey would never feel the impact as defenders tried to stop my momentum towards the end zone. In all honesty I didn't handle the injury well at all, I turned my back on my team, instead of being a positive leader, I failed to attend practices, I stopped communication with my buddies and steered away from the coaches during school. This game was the first time that my team would see me after my injury. I had to hold back tears many times - the coin toss, the horseshoe tradition that we had started and during the game as my friends battled it out trying to hold onto the trophy that we had captured the previous year. The game was close throughout and Greg was an unrelentless cheerleader for the team. As the game came to a close the Brother Andre Cardinals were victorious! I didn't want to hang around more than I had to and wanted to take Greg home right after the game so we started making our way towards the gate on the field. I still had a hobble, however, out of the corner of my eye, I saw my teammates running towards me holding the trophy that came with winning the game. It wasn't long before they surrounded Greg and I and allowed me to share in the moment that they accomplished. Greg felt right at home, he was right in the middle of the team with his hand on the trophy celebrating the victory. Someone took a picture of that moment and you can seeing Greg and I, both in our jerseys, holding up the trophy, treated as if we were on the field the whole game. No one questioned Greg's or my presence holding up the trophy – it was not us who had fought on the field that night, however, we had the prestige honor of hoisting up the victor's prize.

EASILY IMPRESSED

Greg had a way of drawing people's attention. High school was good to Greg and when he arrived I was quick to show him around and check up on him throughout the day. Since I was injured I had nothing but time and was soon known throughout the special needs department as being a friend to Greg. It didn't take Greg long to become a little famous – the kid was cute and was re-united with some of the students that attended his elementary school. I was pretty protective of Greg and although I didn't show it, I would watch, as students would interact with Greg. No matter where Greg went in school there was always someone to say hello to him and Greg loved the attention. The girls were always quick to say hello and give hugs, some of the strangest lines I've heard were, "Greg, don't you remember me? Give me a hug!" "You know if Greg remembered you dear it would have been because you were friends...." Now, Ashley O'Brien and my brother attended the same school and their friends knew Greg quite well but there were groups of kids that I was more skeptical about, especially the guys. You see, a lot of people knew that I was friends with Greg, and that it was a legitimate friendship but the odd person would throw it out there and say that Greg and I were hanging out just so I could look a little more attractive to the girls. I'll tell you right now that it didn't make me any more attractive to the girls, in fact, for the record, I never dated anyone in high school as it was. So I was careful not to feed into any of the potential rumors that others may have held. On the other hand, I was quite observant of other guys who would try to play that card. There were guys who knew Greg from class or from elementary school who had offered a form of superficial acknowledgement. Don't get me wrong, I was an advocate for friendships between students and students with disabilities, what I wasn't an advocate for was how some guys thought that by being cool and calling Greg over during a lunch to their table and saying "Hey Greg, how the F@*& are you" was appropriate. Unfortunately, this happened more often than not. It would come across in whispers, or in actions and most students with disabilities at that age are exposed to so many stimulants in a school setting, add that to trying to fit in and you get one easily impressionable person and Greg was no different!

It didn't take long for me to notice that Greg was mimicking phrases or one-finger salutations that the other students were teaching him. What got to me the most was that these guys who were so quick to pretend that they were friends with Greg at school were nowhere to be found outside of the school walls. It was fine to befriend Greg or any of his friends at school but no one thought to invite these kids with disabilities out after school hours. I called them posers. It all seems jealous and I won't lie, some of it is. I do remember speaking to Jenny about how easily Greg would pick up a bad habit from some of these guys and the work that it would take Jenny to un-teach Greg was unreal. I would observe some of the boys from our school teaching Greg inappropriate gestures and words. Their grasp on Greg's reality unfortunately was limited. They failed to realize that with every bad word and gesture they made Jenny's job and mine a lot harder to undo and explain to Greg what is right and wrong with what he would learn from others. And that is why I was upset.

One event stood out more than others; Greg and I frequented Tim Horton's, especially the one at the corner of 16th and Markham Rd. Usually there were numbers of Brother Andre Students there at any given time and sitting room was a luxury. As Greg and I made our way to the registry, he was being acknowledged by numerous people. I would never rain on his parade and just stayed in line so as to not lose our spot as Greg made his way over to the group calling him. It's funny because in hindsight no one ever asked me why I hung out with Greg. I guess no one thought to ask. When I would bring Greg to a lunch with my friends there was this surprised reaction at first and then the acceptance but high school kids are always a bit immature, right?

Well, as Greg was talking to some people, I ordered his favorite, even still to this day, a small, ice cap with milk! As

I paid for the drinks and turned towards where Greg was, I overheard the boys he was speaking with use a barrage of swear words and tell Greg to kiss one of their girlfriends on the cheek. Boy was I offended – what a bunch of chivalrous bastards I thought. I quickly approached and told Greg that we were leaving and I gather from my tone Greg didn't like what I was demanding, so I said it again and this time he listened. I opened the truck door for Greg and told him to wait there as I went in to speak with the crowd who had gestured to Greg. My Mom will tell you that there isn't much that gets me fired up, I pride myself for the patience that I have and I have a Teflon wall for insults that are directed towards me, however, when there is an injustice that I feel is bona-fide, such as what I saw in Tim Horton's that day, you can believe that I had some words to share with that group. I graciously took the time to explain to them that their behavior was not what Greg should be following and if they ever felt the need to coax Greg into swearing or doing a stupid stunt like kissing a girl he doesn't know, they had another thing coming. I have no idea what that other thing was and I'm just thankful that I never found the same guys pull a stunt like that on my watch again and, believe it or not, one of those guys was enrolled in the 'community arts' class that I took a few years back, and he should have known better!

It was a painstakingly long semester and I was praying for the semester to end faster than it did. I wasn't playing football and I started to put some weight on. The doctor told me that it was in my best interest to try to stay healthy and fit so that I could recover faster after my surgery but I would hear nothing of it. I was borderline depressed and just went through the motion of my days to get them over with. I retreated within myself and closed off many friendships because I couldn't muster the strength to speak with anyone at school. Mom would tell you that I was no gem and at home things weren't that much better. I brought my sadness everywhere I went and couldn't understand why God would allow me to have such an injury in my last year of high school and keep me from playing any sport. Being brought up in a family that serves God, I had turned away from God in the past couple of years as I pursued sports and neglected my relationship with Him. I was angry and a month before surgery my parents recommended that I take Greg for an outing to a youth group held at a church in Markham. I didn't think much of the idea at the time but it gave Greg and me something different to do for once and I put my parent's idea to action.

I was able to drive, however, I still had a pronounced limp. Greg and I arrived at the church and took some seats on the margins of the majority of the group that had assembled in the middle. It appeared to me that most of the kids there had known each other, as the chatter and laughter made them look comfortable. Yet no one welcomed Greg and I that night which I felt to be extremely odd and yet memorable at the same time. Usually, the first thing that happens at a church is that you're welcomed and people can spot out a visitor a mile away – pretty straight forward I would think but that night we went without a welcome. There were a few praise songs before the message and as I was sitting there listening to the words being spoken I couldn't help but think that it was I that this particular sermon was directed towards. Somehow this preacher found out that I was coming and put some words on paper that went directly to my soul. God works that way, He doesn't let his sheep get too far and as in the parable about the lost sheep – He will go looking after the only sheep that strays from the pack.

The words that night talked about how God wants to be the centre of our universe and how easy it is for us to get sidetracked by the world's tactics, finances, accumulation of material things, selfish ambition, work and in my case sports. I couldn't deny that sports undoubtedly took the number one spot in my life and I was guilty of pursuing that over anything else. As the words started to settle in I couldn't hold back the tears as they began to well in my eyes. Greg kept asking why was I crying, and all I could do was cry more. Greg was so kind to put his arm around my shoulders, being a good friend. I re-dedicated my life to the Lord that night and Greg was there with me. You tend to remember events like that quite easily and with those events you tend to recall who was there, words that were spoken and the friend that helped see you through.

CHAPTER TEN

GREG MADE ME A MOVIE

In today's world we are hypnotized to see beauty in very specific ways – more often than not in superficial, fake and idealized ways – to me this is a tragedy.

- Daniel Rossi

Ironically, Andrew during another bowl game the same year that I tore my ACL, tore his while I watched from the sideline. I saw Andrew get hit from behind, and when he didn't get up, immediately I was running on the field to my brother who was sprawled on the ground. Mom used to say that Andrew and I did things in pairs and that he didn't want to be cheated of the chance to tear his knee – same knee by the way. Andrew handled the recovery much better than I did and he was faithful with pre-surgery physiotherapy. Our surgeries were scheduled a week apart and that was so that Mom didn't have to run around looking after both of us at two different times...she wanted to get it over with. I went in on my birthday for the surgery and to this day hate the moment that the anesthesiologist puts the air mask on you and asks you to count down from 10. I have had a bunch of surgeries and trust me it doesn't get any more pleasant. You are at the complete mercy of the surgical staff when you're 'put under' and that can be scary enough.

When I awoke from surgery I was totally incapable of moving my right leg, I felt this dull ache in my leg and even worse I had to PEE...and that was awkward...at the end I needed the assistance of a nurse to complete the task as I felt like it was my first time learning how to pee, oh it was embarrassing. The nurse told me that I had a blood clot form during surgery and that they had to put a tube in from my hip to my shin to drain the blood...the problem was that the tube was still in place and that the next day she was just going to pull it out!!!! "Ya, right", I thought you have to be totally crazy, "you better be putting me under again", I told her!

Mom, Dad and Andrew came to visit me at the hospital that day, they stayed late into the night before they took off, only to return in the morning to take me home. Before I went to bed that night, I had a few reflections. The first was how disappointed I was that no one came to visit me at the hospital. I had surgery on a Saturday, and had loads of friends, or so-called friends tell me that they would come and visit. No one ever did and that made me reconsider what and who my friends were, fortunately the morphine helped me get to sleep that night.

The next day I found myself screaming at the nurse who just pulled the tube out and gave me no warning! I got over it quick, and it was probably the better thing to have happened, rather than her slowly sliding it out from under my skin. I was released shortly after that and soon found myself on the couch in our living room.

Mom had decked out the couch with blankets and pillows as it would be my resting spot for the next week until Andrew went in for his surgery. There's no way of getting comfortable when you don't have the use of one leg, nothing is easy, washing, going to the toilet, changing, sitting. I didn't recognize my body and couldn't get used to working without my leg. I told you that no one came to visit...well no one called either and no one thought to stop by my house as well.

As the night was getting on and I at least started to entertain the fact that I was to be on a couch for a bit, a knock echoed through the living room, Mom jumped to answer the door and when she opened the door it was Jenny O'Brien greeting her on the other side. Jenny was kind and didn't want to interrupt too long, I turned to see her, she sent a wave at me and told me that Greg was in the car and that he was afraid to come in because he didn't like blood and because he didn't want to see me like this. Jenny handed my mom a videocassette that was from Greg. Jenny left soon after and the house was quiet again. Mom had a smile on her face and asked if she could put the cassette in and play it. Sure, it sounds logical but, I don't work that way, when I get a gift, I don't like to open it in front of people, I like to keep cards or letters for when I'm in a quiet space and ready to read the mail or open a gift when no one is around. That hardly happens but when I can that is how I prefer to tend to my mail and gifts. So, I had mom set it up for me, and I would wait until she went to bed before I would play the tape, in private.

When the house was asleep and even the dog was in her bed, I hit 'play' on the remote. I could instantly tell that it was a home video, it started with a clip from the local news station and then changed backgrounds and I was looking at Greg's basement. Greg then walked past the camera; he was dressed in a black suit and had his glasses on. He took a seat behind a little table, and on that table was my old football jersey draped over the ends with a framed picture of Greg, me, and the team captains of the football team holding up the trophy from the win over Father Bressani at the bowl game, and lastly there was a football. It was a little shrine. I still had no idea what he was doing, and didn't expect what I saw next.

Greg introduced the next chapter of his video with "This is for you Dan", and then hit play on his stereo. As the music started to play I couldn't place the tune at first but when Greg started to sing, I knew the song all too well. Greg and I had this habit that when we went out, we would play either Brittany Spears or Backstreet Boys as loud as we could and sing with all of our hearts. Sometimes Greg would look at me and say, "This song is for my friend Daniel Joseph Rossi" and tell me that I wasn't allowed to sing. I would listen and watch as Greg would sing his little heart out and I would just smile. I recognized the words and tears started to roll down my cheeks – I couldn't stop the emotion that was going through me at that moment. Greg sang to me 'I Need You Tonight' by the Backstreet Boys and would add 'I need you tonight – Daniel Rossi' before he would sing the next verse. Greg went on to finish the song and my tears didn't stop for some time after that. I could only watch the video once and at the end of it Greg stood up, thanked me for being his friend, and then called his dad and told him that he was finished! I could only imagine Greg setting up this scene, asking his father, Harold to set the camera up for him, then ask him to leave – sing the song he chose and then with all the innocence in the world call for his dad to turn the camera off when he was done! Thank you Greg and Harold for

103

your combined effort because as innocent as that video was, it proved all the doctors in the world wrong who said children with disabilities learn slower than the rest of the population. Greg was give or take 13-14 years old at the time and knew what the meaning of true friendship was, more so than all the friends I thought I had who promised to come visit me after surgery. Most of us don't even have a grasp on what true friendship is all about, how often do we take the time to let someone know that we are thinking of him or her? It is far too easy to lose touch with someone and play the horrid game of 'well, they know how to contact me, friendship goes both ways'. True enough, but we each can make that decision to pick up a phone, write an e-mail, or these days, send a text message or Facebook someone that we haven't spoken to in a long time and not put it off as though they are the ones that owe it to us to initiate contact. Greg learnt this life lesson years before I did and years before most of the people reading this book.

Experts don't always have it right when it comes to human behavior and especially when it comes to people living with exceptionalities. It is so easy to generalize that people with exceptionalities have difficulties with this and that; I have yet to read of any accounts of what people with exceptionalities do really well. Perhaps this type of logic is the perfect stereotype of society – we constantly focus on the negatives and rarely focus on the positives in life. I'll bring you back to the whole dilemma of the cup is half full (optimists perspective) or the cup is half empty (pessimistic perspective) – I know that you have come across this before, so you are well versed in which side you take your cup on. For years people with exceptionalities have received the short end of the stick and that, I believe is completely wrong. I won't argue with some facts and statistic that have been published by recognized experts, what I will argue is that the majority of these experts fail to incorporate the human factor in their publications and works. The human factor as per my definition would be the resilience to surpass any amount of expectation or challenges whether inherent or implied because we are beautifully created in the likeness of God and each of us has something valuable to offer this world. We all contain this human factor within ourselves, it might be coated with other priorities, or goals, but it's there and it wants to make this world a better place and I'm not simply saying through donating money.

Absolutely, we need people to donate money to support the thousands of causes and organizations out there, but the world isn't changed when you or I donate $20.00 here and there. Change doesn't happen until we personalize the change we want to see in the world, whether that is poverty – manifested in multiple ways, the pandemic of AIDS, or environmental concerns. When you personalize a cause, you connect with that cause and your actions become more meaningful and money becomes a secondary asset.

MOVING ON

I barely graduated high school, it wasn't because I was a horrible student, it was because I was so upset that I was not able to play sports that I tried very little academically. The repercussions were significant, if I were to go to university I had to wait two years so I could apply as a mature student and in that way I would only need my grade 13 English mark for a qualifier.

Most of the people I spoke with warned me about taking two years off before continuing with my education – most said that I wouldn't go back, that I would get used to the money and not think twice about school, and so on and so forth. Mom and Dad knew that I would go back and that's what counts, right? I knew I would go back as well and that had to count for something. People are always quick to give their opinions and most times those opinions are by-products of a person's ideology in which they have a formed opinion about and it is their duty to share it with others.

I can't divulge too much about what happened in those two years, because that will be another book for another time. What I will share with you is a brief synopsis and with a focus on my time spent in Canada.

I wanted to travel, more importantly I wanted to volunteer overseas as my travel experience, I wanted to be immersed with different cultures, learn different ways of life, see sunsets in places I couldn't have imagined, eat with local people, and provide some form of service that brought value to the communities and peoples that I encountered. For those two years I wanted to stay around home during the Christmas season food bank that my family ran out of the Salvation Army. Mom would always say that it was hard to find good help, and she could always count on me for providing that good help that she needed. So, as a result I would generally travel after Christmas and ensure that I was back in time to work and make money in the summer construction season.

All that wasn't enough, both years from September to November I accepted a coaching position from the newly acquired head coach of my former football team, the Brother Andre Cardinals. I was asked to coach the junior boy's defensive team and I was honored and excited to take on the challenge.

My brother Andrew was on the senior team and was playing offence that year and we were sharing the same field so I could always have an eye on him. The Cardinals had fully recovered from that strike when I was in grade 11 and now the team returned to two separate teams, one junior and the other senior. I told Greg about my new title and he was ecstatic, probably more so than I was, his first request was that he help me coach and with pleasure I said yes!

Before the season started Greg and I would play 'Madden 01', a football game that I had on a game system I rarely played. From the game we could pick plays that we thought were good and come up with names for them. Now these meetings that Greg and I held were not serious by any means, they most likely lasted a couple of minutes, before we would discuss the next big idea, whatever that was.

When I started with the team, a few of the grade 10 players had been on my team the year previous, and had an idea of who I was, or at least had heard about who I was. The grade 9 players were new to me and new to football and knowing that the grade 10's weren't able to get much playing time the year previous on a varsity team I had my work cut out for me.

My first priority was to establish my expectations for the season, that being based on character, teamwork and hard work ethic. Right off the bat I made it clear that it was unacceptable for our defense to receive a penalty for unsportsmanlike conduct during a game or during a practice. I resorted to leading by example and the two weeks of training camp was solely focused on physical conditioning, team building skills and understanding the game of football. Most of these kids had no idea what football was all about and as it stood 9 of the 12 starting players for the defense had never played football before, I only had one substitute for the entire squad and by default he had to know every position!

We would start every practice with a prayer, and end every practice with a five minute open mike session so the players could voice any concerns or share ideas. Mostly I would explain about the balance that I wanted each of them to maintain in life as they played football and not make the same mistake as me and put the sport above everything and I mean everything!

I would do all the drills with the kids, I would lead the runs, I would sweat and fall, I would get down in the mud when I had to, and I would do the push-ups I assigned to the whole squad when they made a mistake. I would never single out an individual, but challenged the whole team and punished all 13 players and not just the one guilty for any mistake. I thrived on being a leader through example and didn't want the young squad to think they could get away with half-hearted practices and effort just because I was a young coach. The squad learned fast and we shared a great relationship.

When I was a player for the Cardinals, there were two personal goals that I had each season, one was the obvious championship game, and the other was the most prestige bowl game against our biggest rivals, the Markham Marauders from the public school a 5-minute drive from our home turf. A huge crowd would gather without fail each year, and alumni from both teams would come and watch their predecessors engage in a battle for the games trophy. I would like to tell you that the Cardinals held more victories than the Marauders, but unfortunately that is not so. Markham consistently put forth a strong team and they held the title of arch nemeses ever since I could remember. During my tenure at Brother Andre, we beat Markham once and that was early in my career when I was in grade nine and we were never able to accomplish the feat again.

Back to the junior team that I was coaching. There were three games before we met the Marauders in the bowl game and we fell short in each of those games. The games were close and it was largely a shortcoming on our offensive team to score touchdowns. Proudly I could say that an inexperienced defensive squad would hold their own against their larger opponents and hold them to two scores, if that, for most of our games. It was frustrating falling to what I perceived to be the worst of the teams in the league and then going into our biggest bowl game without a win made me a little nervous. Before the game I shared my thoughts with the team and expressed my aspirations of wanting to beat Markham, in the 'Markham Cup' when I had played and only getting to feel the satisfaction once in my five years at school. I told the team that no matter what happened I expected nothing less than for each of them to have fun and try their best. I used to have the team sing this rugby song that I learnt over the years. It was starting a bit of a new tradition away from the horseshoe, but it was effective. It didn't match up to the New Zealand All Blacks Haka dance that they would perform before their rugby matches for intimidation and unity, but it did catch the attention of our opponents every time. It was intimidating in its own right and when the whole team sang the chant, it drew attention from all who watched and in my opinion made the other team look unorganized. The chant was lead by one of the captains, the rest of the team would surround the captain and they would start off in a whisper.

"Ooo – ale ale and then the rest of the team repeated after every verse – 'alea ticki, tonga – a wasa wasa wasa – ooo ale aluae alua – the chant would escalate after every chorus until the team was yelling the chant! I never inquired about what the words meant, but it did sound good when 25 plus players would perform the ritual before they took the field.

With the defense, it was known that I would not accept a missed tackle and before each game I would hold a one-on-one tackle drill so if there was to be a missed tackle it would be prior to the game and not throughout. Some people thought that I was crazy as my squad would get their clean uniforms dirty as they tackled each other before the game but it worked I can assure you! Mom had brought Greg to the game and he was standing close to the sideline eagerly cheering the team on. The Markham team that year had defeated their previous opponents by unheard of numbers, some teams fell by 7 or 8 scores, and we had yet to manage more than two scores in a single game. As Markham took the field I got a feeling like no other. It's one thing to take the field as a player, running in front of the cheering crowd and standing on the field before it became an arena of tactics and struggle, but as a coach I felt something different. I was years younger than the Markham coaches and I felt a responsibility for the squad of boys that I had trained leading up to the game. I felt as though they were a reflection of me on the field, they would take what I shared with them, add their own talent and somehow it was a testament to the work that was invested in them and let them roam. I felt as though I wasn't just playing against the Markham

Marauders offense, but I was playing against their coaching staff and that perspective made the game that much more special. When I was a player, I focused on beating the team, never factored in the coaching staff and now I felt that the coaching staff was very much a part of the equation.

As the game was played out, I had chewed through most of my nails and cannot tell you how many times I was shocked when my squad would stop the Marauders rolling offense. Greg was on the sideline yelling different plays for me to call! I had to tell him to keep it quiet because I didn't want the other team to know what our plays were! As half time sounded and the players went to their respective benches the score read that the Marauders were only up by 6 points. I was ecstatic, the defense was holding the league's highest scoring team to a dismal 6 points and those points came through two field goals and not a touchdown! I didn't have much to say to my squad, except keep their heads up and keep playing the way they were.

At the time I liked to think that I revolutionized the way that high school football was played defensively. I had players going in motion, switching positions, and calling out what the offensive formation looked like throughout the game, all in an effort to confuse the offensive players who generally would look at the same defensive formation at that level. With the constant movement of my defense, the offence couldn't adjust in time and often I would see two or three offensive players just standing around during a play looking for someone to block – that alleviated three extra players on my squad to stop the ball movement! It was magnificent! We shut them down all game and at the sound of the final whistle the game ended in a 6 all draw. I must have celebrated as if my team had just won the super bowl of the NFL. The Markham coaches were in disbelief, and even more so when my team pranced around the field as though they were victorious in the match. In a draw the team that held the bowl coming into the match retained the title. It didn't matter to us though; a draw with the best team in the league was a win for us! Greg was right there in the middle of the celebration and on the drive home that night we stopped at the local Tim Horton's and had a post celebratory ice cap – Greg was dressed in his Cardinals jersey and probably would have signed autographs if anyone had asked!

We lost all the other games that season but finished the season with a whole lot more experience than when we started. I was excited for the next season even though it was 12 months away. As a portion of the team's out of football character building skills, I made it mandatory for all the players on the defense to volunteer at the food bank that I helped run if they wanted to start the next year. At this point Greg was not new to the food bank and had attended at least a couple of years now. Greg was pre-dictable when he stepped foot into our warehouse, he would head over to the toy section before the start of his shift. He wanted to see what was new and if there were any wrestler figurines that he could play with and further ask for as Christmas presents. It was fun watching as Greg would make his rounds throughout the food bank, he was a fan favorite of all the women that volunteered there, and they would call on Greg to help them with any task at hand that they were working on. I would always have a special job for Greg to do, every year, I would pack a cou-ple of boxes for Greg and tell him that it was his respon-sibility to put all the items in the box in their proper spots. Everything was labeled and spread out throughout the warehouse, and it was Greg's job to find where each item went. I would give him an assortment of food and toys that needed to be sorted and then he would be off to work. Throughout Greg's time there I would watch him when I could and I would see a strict determination as he would grab an item from his box, figure out what it was and then try to find the appropriate location it was to go. Greg would mind his own business, finish his job and then almost like clockwork ask if we could go get an Ice Cap!!

The year that I hosted my football players I didn't have the time to put a box together for Greg to sort through during his shift. While I was explaining the ins and outs of the food bank to the players and assigning different tasks I saw Greg out of the corner of my eye, just like the players Greg was wearing his football jersey, #31. Greg had taken it upon himself to find a box and start sorting through the items in the box and finding their rightful locations. The team broke to their different duties and I stood where I was and admired my friend as he became a leader and didn't wait to be directed to work and took it upon himself to find a job. Greg was my number one man when it came to making sure the team behaved themselves at the food bank. Greg would keep the guys in check for me and would report any ill behavior that would result in the players doing push-ups. It was a way of making sure they stayed in shape during the off-season and that as young boys they didn't get carried away with language or inappropriate behavior. In all honesty they weren't that bad, I was just playing it up.

CHAPTER ELEVEN

INTERNATIONAL ASPIRATIONS

*To travel is to discover that everyone
is wrong about other countries.*

- Aldous Huxley

In the Simien Mountains - Ethiopia

As I planned my trips abroad, I would have a special dinner with Greg before I would leave. Jenny would always caution me about not allowing him to eat too much because without quality control, the boy could keep eating and not stop! I had the privilege of traveling to various places and exploring a world around me that was full of vibrancy and culture. I was fascinated with travelling to developing world countries partly because they were more affordable to travel to and they held the opportunities that I was hoping to experience. The time I spent overseas opened the door to a different spectrum of poverty. I have expressed that poverty is manifested in many forms; there is social poverty, which exists when we deprive those around us by not sharing our most precious commodity, that being our time! When I was overseas I saw different forms of poverty. I saw the familiar images of villages with children walking around, malnourished, I saw the shanty towns that were impromptu housing works that held families, open pit latrines that filled the air with grotesque aroma's and life that appeared to be dim and hopeless in comparison to mine. Regardless, of where I traveled I was able to experience a form of kindness that I have rarely felt in the comforts of North America. I experienced a welcoming from families that had very little, but would share the little they had with me. Families would host me for a dinner and I would sit at their table and watch as they brought out the best of their possessions to the table. I never asked for anything but was able to share in the best that those I met had to share with me, it was impressionable on my heart and I vowed to remember this form of love and kindness that came through regardless of the unyielding poverty surrounding the lives of people I shared it with.

BACK IN ACTION

After a summer of travel, football season was on the horizon and I was anticipating another exciting round with the Junior boy's football team. Most of the returning players had played for me the year before and had a foundation of understanding for the game. Greg and I sat down over an ice cap prior to the season and discussed names for the plays that we dreamt up. Some of my favorites were 'little giants', 'house of pain', 'sky blitz' and 'rock-em'. The best part was that the team welcomed the imagination and effort that we put into the calls that we would use all season.

Because most of the players were returning, there was no time wasted with the opening camp that year for the defense. I couldn't understand it but I still only had one extra player for the entire defense, and for the life of me I could never remember his birth name and resorted to calling him, 'Hershey Squirt'. Hershey, was small and wasn't the most talented on the team, but the one thing that I liked about Hershey was that he had the heart of a lion and came to every practice willing to give his all. I promised myself to let Hershey start at least once that year. I had to reward his hard work ethic and enthusiasm that he brought to every practice.

I kept the same coaching style as the year previous, the rapport that I held with the players was respectful and positive, it was a learning environment for all of us and I wanted to keep it that way. Every coach has a different style of how they approach their teams, we've all had good coaches and my style was unique to who I was. I didn't hold the same coaching experience as the other coaches for the Junior boy's football team, but I was the most popular, and I would like to think that it was because of how I engaged my team beyond the game of football.

One of the first practices that I held, Greg came out to help me coach. Because there were only 13 players on defense it was difficult to have any kind of offence versus defense drills incorporated in our practices. I told the team about Greg coming out, and most of the players were in the same grade as Greg was at the time and welcomed the idea. My plan was to have Greg and I play offence against the team and told the players to fall when I would hand the ball off to Greg and let him reach the end zone untouched! Déjà-vu set in as I became the quarter back and Greg the receiver, we had done this before, just the two of us, with only imaginary defenders we played as if we were under Friday night lights in front of thousands of cheering fans. Except this time, we were up against the Junior boy's football team.

'Down, set HUT', I quickly handed the ball off to Greg and watched as he scampered down the field, players fell off his path and Greg ran it in for the score! It took a while to get Greg comfortable enough to work with the team that practice, for the majority of the session he stood beside me or close to the sideline and was content with just watching. I would go over to encourage him to get more involved, and he would get nervous and withdrawn and pull away from me. Finally, it was the team that helped get him involved and I think we all valued watching Greg run for a score against 12 defenders that lay scattered on the field.

The first game of the season held us victorious over our opponents, it was my first win as a coach and it felt good to have won a game. It had rained that game and there was a sinkhole that lay on the outskirts of the field and I promised the boys that if we won, I would be the first to slide through the puddle, and I owned up to the promise.

Our record was even as we entered our bowl game against the Markham Marauders. The atmosphere before the game was a mixture of excitement and intensity. I reminded the team about the previous year's accomplishments against the best team in the league, and this year was no different, Markham held an undefeated record and was the leader of the league. We had home-field advantage, and took the field with pride in our red Cardinal jerseys. The year previous proved my philosophy of a rapid evolving defensive front, one that was constantly shifting and confusing our opponents and in that regard we played with the same tactics. The only difference this year was that I incorporated elaborate hand gestures to the plays that were designed.

I relished the feeling of being on the field, even though I wasn't playing I felt more a part of the team than ever before. To give you an idea about the Markham coaching staff, before the start of the game I headed to their sideline to wish them good luck and it was met with an empty stare and no response. Traditionally, you see handshakes and congratulations at the end of the game, not before, and I wanted to mix it up a bit, I had a good feeling about this game and wanted them to know that I'd be too busy afterwards for a handshake! And I had never been more right than I was at that moment. When the game started, the team let the Markham Marauders know that they meant business! Football experts often say that games are won and lost on the backs of the defense and that couldn't have been truer that game as my boys took the field. With the game tied going into the half, I couldn't have been more proud of my squad. Once again they were shutting down the high scoring offense of the Markham Marauders and I loved every minute of it, especially the frustration that their coaching staff was displaying on the sidelines.

The last half of the game was the most exciting and will remain in my memories forever. With the game tied and Markham on our 20 yard line looking to score, the quarter back handed the ball off to their tailback, I saw him elude one tackle, then another but was quickly met by the Cardinals outside linebacker, a grade 10 student that hit him so hard that the tailback crumpled to the ground, at the same time dropping the ball. Every practice I would teach the defense that any ball left on the ground was a live ball and I expected them to jump on it and gain control. I would often drop a ball every now and then to see who was paying attention and would get half a dozen players jumping for the ball at any given point. As the ball was rolling in the ground and me yelling for someone to grab it, my defensive tackle scooped up the ball and turned his head towards the Marauders end zone. Defensive tackles are not known for their speed or quickness, but that boy ran like I have never seen before. As he was crossing the yard markers I was elated, his path was 10 yards from our sideline and we could see his engine pumping as he ran towards us and the end-zone. The team on the sideline with all their might was cheering him on and we were all lost in the moment of cheering. Then right in front of us a blue jersey appeared from nowhere and had caught up to the steaming cardinal engine of my defensive tackle and jumped on his back. Now, there are reasons why people play the positions they do in football – the fast boys are usually the receivers or running backs, the medium solid built boys are linebackers and the bigger boys take either an offensive blocking position or defensive rushing – either way they do not have much practice running or controlling the ball. As the Markham defender closed the distance I started to yell for my defensive tackle to secure the ball and hold on tight - my warning was too late, as the Marauder jumped on the back of our steaming engine, the ball was easily discharged and bounced to the ground as the two boys dropped one on top of the other.

Oh, the temptation...the ball was right in front of me since I was following the play...all I had to do was pick it up and run it into the end zone myself! The only thing I can equate it to would be a scenario in where you haven't eaten for days, you're starving, and then someone places your favorite meal right in front of you and tells you that if you resist the meal you'll get another reward...but fail to tell you what that reward is – you fight your body to not eat, but the temptation is too great, and the thought of another reward tells you that it might be worth the wait... what a dilemma!

I taught my boys many lessons about the game of football, positioning, tackling, reading plays and at that moment in time I was thinking about nothing else other than diving for that ball myself, and forgot that one of the most important lessons I taught the boys was about to happen. 'When you recover a fumble or get an interception during the game, I don't want everyone to stand around and watch as their team mate runs it back until he is stopped, I want the rest of you running behind him, blocking, and available for a lateral if need be!' The ball wasn't on the ground long when another Cardinal jersey appeared, and in one motion scooped down, picked up the ball and ran it straight into the end zone!!!! The best part was that the rest of the team was following and as they were in the end zone sharing that moment I struggled holding back the tears that were welling up in my eyes. We had the lead with 5 minutes to play and I knew that this was the year that I would beat Markham.

When the excitement died down, I told my tired defensive squad that they had to get back out there and do it one more time as Markham had one more chance to play offence. The Marauders were hungry for a score, and it didn't take them long to return into scoring position with time ticking down on the clock.

Football can be an emotional sport, when you have the lead you're elated, when the score is close, you're focused and when the other team is in scoring position to tie the game, you're nervous. With no time outs left the Marauders quarterback threw a 15 yard score to his receiver and brought the score within one point. When you score in football you have two options, you can kick a field goal for a single point or you can attempt to score a two-point conversion either by running or throwing a pass in for a score. I was on my toes – the sheer closeness of the game made my stomach turn, I looked over to the Marauders bench and saw their coach holding up two fingers, indicating that he wanted his team to go for the two point conversion and the win. This meant that the Marauders would be placed on the 5-yard line with one final attempt to seal the game.

I can't even remember what play I called for the defense to form in for the final barrage. When the ball was brought back to the quarterback, he faked a handoff – known as a play action pass, the idea is to suck the defense in thinking it is a run, hit the running back who wouldn't have the ball, but that opened up a receiver if the defender playing safety, releases his coverage, then the quarter back just has to throw an easy pass to the open receiver. I saw the fake and was yelling that it was a pass, knowing all too well that my words were falling on determined ears. As the Marauders quarterback was rolling out, looking for his open receiver, I dreaded the moment of uncertainty as to whether my team all committed to the fake and would have left that receiver open. The clock was at zero, the ball went up in the air, I saw the Marauder receiver deep in the end zone as the ball was floating towards him, a set of hands came up and met the ball and clasped down on the pigskin, my safety wasn't fooled by the play action pass and had intercepted the ball for a roller coaster ending to the game! The entire team erupted when the buzzer went off, and the score was 14-13 for the Cardinals – I ran onto the field to join the squad not able to hold back my inexpressible joy as we became victorious. In all the chaos of the victory I didn't realize that the team's attention turned to me, and they circled around me as though I was the one that made the game winning score and hoisted me up on their shoulders and carried me around the field. I didn't register what was being done until it was all over. We almost forgot to collect the trophy; I was a bit embarrassed to be carried around by the team, as my fellow coaches stood on the sidelines watching but I did tell you that I was the most popular coach on the team! I never had the chance to shake the hands of the Markham Marauder coaches, but I wasn't too bothered by that, I did give them the opportunity before the game, after all.

In the end, the boys did it, they made my dream come true, they allowed me to beat the Markham Marauders in the 'Markham Cup' something that I desperately wanted when I was a player and was not able to achieve, but as a coach I lead my former team to victory over our arch rivals.

This small victory taught me a valuable lesson. Throughout high school I continually put football first in my life; I lived, breathed and thought football all the time. I placed football above my family and God and that turned out to be a mistake. God is a jealous God, and when I got hurt I was quick to blame Him for my injury and depression. What I failed to do was stop and listen to what He was trying to tell me. God was telling me that he had other plans in store for me that went well beyond the playing fields of football and into the path of people and places that I could have never imagined coming across.

God lets us live our dreams and share in the moments that are placed on our heart – God knew that when I was a player for the Brother Andre Cardinals I wanted to hold up the trophy after beating the Markham Marauders in the 'Markham Cup', and when the time was right, he allowed me to share in that moment, but it was on his time and not mine. I vowed not to put anything or anyone in front of God from that moment on and be open to the course in life that I was pre-destined to walk.

God doesn't ask us to tip-toe in our belief or un-belief of Him – its either 'yes' or 'no', one or the other. When you say 'yes' you are entering a friendship in which you will look at your life and allow God to infuse His love for others in it and be able to make a difference in every situation that you are placed in. That may sound like fluffed up words that are impossible to live by and I'll be the first to admit that I fail in comparison, however, I know that every situation I encounter, whether good or bad, God has a reason behind it and there is always someone who may be in a situation who might just need a smile or a simple hello and that simple gesture could make the world of difference in that moment.

It is impossible for us to be absent of time, we can plan for the future, but the future is not for us to hold, we only have control of today and the moments that we are in, the future is a foresight to plan for, but can change in the blink of an eye. This story about winning a football game is menial – I probably remember it more than anyone I coached that year and as time goes on, the trophy that was hoisted that game will rust and hardly be remembered by others, it will sit in a trophy case somewhere until years have passed and memory of its past glory are completely absent. But the lesson that I walked away with from that game cannot be described any better than what the apostle Peter, spoke of in his 2 book. "But do not forget this one thing, dear friends: with the Lord a day is a like a thousand years, and a thousand years are like a day. The Lord is not slow in keeping his promise, as some under-stand slowness. He is patient with you, not wanting any-one to perish, but everyone to come to repentance." My short-lived football career taught me this – in God's time I was able to live out a dream and cherish it more than I could have ever imagined.

The Junior Boy's football team finished the rest of the season with a winning record, and more notably having beaten all the best teams in the league. I couldn't have been any prouder of the squad that I was involved with. The boy's season was a memorable one, and when we entered our last game of the season, a game that would decide if we would have an opportunity to compete in the playoffs, I was reminded of my promise that I made to let Hershey play. Up until now, Hershey sat every game on the side line, for two years, he had not seen the field during a game and when all of our games were close in score, in addition with none of my players being injured, Hershey, the only substitute for the defense never had the chance to play.

As I posted the starting line-up the practice before the game I immediately received arguments from the other coaches (my former teachers) about the decision. It wasn't a secret that despite the size of Hershey's heart, it was his physical size and lack of skill that was the big-ger stumbling block to him starting and playing in such an important game. I was out-numbered, and enraged that I was being questioned from men that I respected. I knew the game meant a lot and I also knew that keeping my promise meant a lot to me. Remember that you are never in the wrong when you do what is right. On paper I let the coaches have their way, I erased Hershey's name from the starting roster, and avoided eye contact with the little guy, knowing all too well that he would once again put on a splendid effort on the sideline as he cheered for his team.

Before the game, I pulled over one of my hardest hitting linebackers. This gladiator was only in grade 9 and I knew that with his talent he could have started for the senior team if he wanted to, and I also knew that he had another year of junior football the year after. The favor I asked was huge and I trusted that I had asked the right player to take on the task. With both my hands on his shoulder, I made this statement,

'After your first tackle, I want you to stay down and clutch your ankle, roll around on the ground and scream in agony – I'll run out with the trainer and I want you to say that you think it's your ankle and you can't move it and in your spot I'm going to play Hershey for the rest of the game.'

I don't know if I can honestly say that if I were in the same position I would have agreed to what was being asked of me. However, I was not disappointed, just liked planned, after the first play from scrimmage, my middle linebacker went down rolling and holding his ankle! As promised I ran onto the field with the trainer, took the helmet off the player and was impressed by how he played his 'injury'. He and I were the only two that knew it was a hoax, and when the trainer and I stood him up and he placed his arms around our shoulders and hobbled off the field both teams started clapping their support. When we approached the sideline, my player was grabbing the wrong ankle; the trainer took note and asked him what the deal was? The lie was brilliant enough to have her believe that he was still injured and he would stay on his backside the remainder of the game with an ice pack on an ankle that was as healthy as an ox.

The referee gave me another 20 seconds to re-align and send out the replacement player. I looked down the sideline and amidst all the large players I saw Hershey, helmet on, mouth guard dangling and watching the players on the field with no idea what I was about to do! "Hershey", I used the military voice for the call out, "Come here", it took Hershey a second to realize what I was doing. When he was in front of me I stooped down, grabbed his facemask and asked if he was ready! I believed that the little man had no idea what he was doing, and when I sent him in with the play, I had 11 players looking at me from the field with no idea what call Hershey was supposed to bring out!

There he was, by far the smallest player amongst the giants, and I actually worried about his safety although it was short-lived. After Hershey's first play, I soon found him running off! "Hershey, it's only been one play, what are you tired?" I inquired. Hershey told me that another player had replaced him, something that went under my radar, as I had no idea. The other coaches took it upon themselves to place one of their offensive players, who had never played defense in Hershey's spot, simply because they thought their choice was a better athlete. I was furious, how could my so-called colleagues be so ignorant! I called a time-out, and called out the offensive player that had just gone out. When the other coaches asked why I called a time-out I was quick to tell them that, "Hershey is going back in!" They were quick to attack my decision; in front of the team they shared their true colors. "He will lose the game for us if we put him in, and the other team will run it through his gap the whole game and take advantage of his size!"

I could not believe the honesty that they portrayed in front of the team – a whole season of coaching the defense and never had they challenged any of my decisions or tactics and now on the brink of the playoffs, they were assuming control of the squad that responded to my commands. The head coach, who rarely came to our junior games and in my opinion was not a leader to be followed, claimed control of defense and told me to watch the rest of the game. I had it out with the coaches in front of the entire team; I stood up for Hershey and could not believe the words that these leaders spoke in front of their players and students. The referees and the other team were dumbfounded and had no idea what was going on our sideline. I stood down, only out of respect for my elders and the team that had to witness this outrageous decision. I was on the sideline for a total of 5 plays – unrenowned to the coaching staff the defensive playbook that they provided me at the start of the year to teach the kids never left my closet. All the plays that we used were the plays that Greg and I came up with on napkins and loose-leaf paper at Tim Horton's ☺. So, when the head coach took over, and started to call plays that his senior team knew and had expected the junior team to know the game turned into a disaster when the players stood on the field with no idea what calls were being sent in through hand signals. The defense let up a touchdown and for the first time since I took over in two years walked off the field with their head down.

The team had a somber spirit amongst them, and the head coach was frustrated in only 5 plays and a touchdown. His rant accused them of not knowing their plays and proper positioning. The plays he was referring to fell on deaf ears, I had never taught the plays designed by the head coach. The squad responded well to our plays and knew them off by heart and never needed a playbook that in my opinion was designed for higher level players and less fun! The defensive captain voiced his response, "Coach Rossi, never taught us those plays, he taught us his own plays and that's all we know." The head coach turned numerous shades of red, and had no other option but to ask me back into the game to resume my coaching position. I was humiliated in front of the team; I was overridden with illogical power, I was asked to step down because I stood up for what I believed in and for a promise that I had made. All I could think about when I stepped away from the team was leaving, packing up my equipment, jumping in my truck and taking off. Thankfully I had more invested into the team than the other coaches ever could – in that time all I could remember thinking were the words spoken by the apostle Paul in his instruction for his young prentice, "Don't let anyone look down on you because you are young, but set an example for the believers in speech, in life, in love, in faith and in purity" (1 Timothy 4:11-13). I was not about to let ignorance and pride win the battle that day, I resumed control of the team, and immediately put Hershey back in to the threat of "if we lose the game it's because you put that kid in", from the head coach. "You have to be joking," I thought, I held my tongue and prayed that Hershey wouldn't let me down and further prove the coaches wrong in their speech and thoughts.

After all the commotion had settled and the defense took the field again, Hershey took his position in the middle of the pack. I thought if I put him in the middle then he would have more support from his teammates if he missed a tackle.

Finally the game was resuming! The ball was hut, the quarterback dropping back, he faked a hand-off, looking for an open receiver, and just as he was about to throw the ball, our little Hershey hit the quarterback from the blindside and caused him to drop the ball, and just like I taught the boys, at least six of them must have jumped on the pigskin! The squad ran off the field excited and giving me a high five as they passed. Hershey brought up the rear of the squad and when he stopped in front of me, sweat beading off his face, gasping for air, smile on his face – a couple of tears from me told him I was proud. Hershey would go on to play the rest of the game, and was ferocious, he led the team in tackles that game, the opponents tried to take advantage of his size and run the ball his direction but would be stopped every time. Even when Hershey didn't hit the ball carrier, they would either trip over his sprawling body, or Hershey's teammates were quick to the rescue. The decision to play Hershey paid off and I can only hope that wherever Hershey is, that he remembers that game for the rest of his life and the impact that he made.

That was my last game as the Junior Boy's defensive coach; the boys didn't make the playoffs that year, but had a winning record and with pride could say they beat the best teams in the league. I didn't speak much with the coaching staff after that game, nor did I feel the need too. I held a great relationship with the team and that is what makes a difference to me at the end of the day.

At the end of the season I asked the team to write a brief letter of what they had learned that season and what they learned about themselves. I collected the letters at the team dinner and took an evening to read the words my players had to share. I was surprised and impressed with the comments that I read – I went the whole season without fully knowing the growth that the players were going through, what they learned and how they were going to bring those skills and qualities into the next season.

I accepted enrollment at a post-secondary institute starting the year after and knew that I wouldn't have been able to join the boys in their last year of junior football. My dreams had come true, and to God I was joyfully thankful, it saddened me that I would not be there to coach the boys in a season in which they would go on to win, not just the league, but win their way to the provincial championship game and lose by 5 points in that endeavor. I couldn't have been any more proud of a group of boys that knew nothing of football when I met them during our first season, won their first game and beat all the best teams during our second season together; then go on to become champions in their third.

I would leave class when the boys were in their playoff run, and watch them from the sidelines of the various playing fields that they fought over. I would smile when they could come out singing the song that I taught them, and before they entered their divisional championship game, I snuck into their change room when the other coaches had left, and told them how proud I was of their accomplishments, and to go out and play the best game of their life – and remember every moment of it.

CHAPTER TWELVE

A CALL TO LEAD

*'Let us not love in word and talk but
in action and truth' 1 John 3:18*

**-The Five with Drive Foundation
Mission Statement**

*Andrew and I in Kenya – We partnered
with our first school in Nairobi*

Mom, Dad and Andrew were all huddled around our kitchen counter when I placed into a hat all the post-secondary schools that I was accepted to inside. "Alright, Dad, say a prayer and the school I pick is the one that I'm going to", I said without hesitation. Dad said a prayer; I put my hand into the hat and pulled out, the University of Guelph. Without a moment of recourse about the school that I was going to, I was accepted into their international development program. I started University at the age of 22, and was 4 years older than the cohort that started school with me at the time. Not only did I prove all the skeptics wrong who said I would never go back, I ended up returning to school when Ontario dropped their OAC (or grade 13) program and entered university with 'kids' who could have easily passed as my campers from my previous life – it was known as the 'double cohort'.

The month prior to starting this new chapter in my life, I decided to go travelling with Andrew around the United Kingdom. The trip was phenomenal and the trouble we got into was worth the experience of the adventure with my younger brother. The only problem with our travel plans was that the school was inundated with new students and because I was not around to answer their copious amount of distress calls saying that I did not get the 'senior' residence buildings that I had requested and they regretted to inform me that I was going to the international house of the campus. It wasn't my first choice, and I didn't care to argue over the issue of where I would lay my head down.

I am not the person to overreact to many situations, I'm passionate but don't show it often, it takes a lot to fire me up, I don't get over excited about things and I don't tend to use the words..."I love", before describing an experience or my favorite foods. I am as easy as they come, and thrive on the secrecy of the activities I involve myself with, not wanting to boast about who I think I am or what I do to make this world a better place. That's a sufficient introduction to how I approached university – there were loads of stories and trouble that I straight out dove into, but those stories are for another day and another time.

Simply maintaining the 'status quo' is not my type of thing. The word is described as – maintain the state of affairs. To me that means, that you become comfortable in your surroundings, comfortable within the realms of your bubble and go through the motions, day in and day out of a set routine. University was exactly that for me – I saw students, stuck in a status quo of routine, albeit a positive and constructive routine of adult based learning and experimentation, but a routine nonetheless. The problem with routine is that if you are not careful it can curb your creative usefulness and ability to function outside of where your comfort zone allows. Thousands of students to me, did the same thing day in and day out at university and it was predictable; go to class, study, eat, class, eat, a bit of study, some form of gossip, video games (if you are a male), eat, party on the weekends.

I found it extremely difficult to settle into a routine that had that as its main structure. I'm not saying that all student life resembles this brief description, however, you couldn't argue that the greater part of the time spent at school saw the majority of the campus adhere to something similar to what I described.

Since, I was and have been, more aligned to what I will call the 'status rev', which I interpret as, the status revolution. It's a state that recognizes what the status quo holds, it identifies those that are content with the current state, but then it revolutionizes the present to a more elaborate occurrence of events and interjects life into the mix. My 'status rev' started the second day at school – right off the bat I became a big brother with the *Big Brothers Big Sisters of Guelph* because Andrew became one and I was intrigued with the organization and how they provided mentors to young children who are lacking a role model in their life, and I wanted to share my time with a kid that needed a friend to look up to. I also made the rugby team. However, more importantly I decided to act on a dream that I came across three months before I started school. That dream would define the course of action for my first year of university and subsequently the years that followed.

Ever since working with the food bank at a young age, I constantly wanted to 'make a difference' in the lives of those that I came across. Andrew and I, along with three other friends the summer prior to university went on an 85 km hike taking the Bruce Trail from Hamilton to Niagara Falls. Outdoor life was nothing new to my friends or me – Andrew and I were in Scouts as kids and since I was in the army, every other weekend was spent outdoors under the night sky. As we plotted away through our hike, it came to pass at one of our campfires that we discussed the crazy idea of hiking the Great Wall of China.

I don't know what girls are like, but boys can go off on some very strange tangents and laugh at events that are so illogical and unlikely that only a boy could create in their minds. The conversation did hold some ultraistic intent – the group of five of us, thought that it would be neat to engage in an event that was unique and distinct, an event that no one has attempted before and a chance to make a little bit of history. I am extremely thankful that the majority of my friends all have a sense of dreaming, which makes it easy for me – an instigator – to play off from. When the trip was over, I immediately did some research, I figured out the Great Wall of China was 6,400 kilometers in length and if we averaged 50 kilometers a day, potentially we could complete the trek in 128 days if all went well and there were no injuries or environmental catastrophes. Then there was the whole aspect of logistical coordination, per-mission from Chinese authorities, safety while on the wall, GPS tracking devices for supporters to follow, sponsorship, food and the list went on and on. What was discussed as a grand idea soon became a daunting task. The five of us figured that the project was out of our league and the amount of planning and coordination that would have had to go into such an event could not be managed by our overloaded personal schedules. We all settled on the fact that it was an awesome idea that none of us had the time to complete.

Despite our agreement not to pursue our over ambitious talk of walking the Great Wall of China, I still enjoyed the idea of doing something unique – an event that was different in comparison to the events of a single person traversing an incomprehensible journey supporting a cause in the name of charity. Knowing that the friends who spoke excitedly of challenging themselves into something that none of us had done up until that point, made me think that if I could think of something that did not require as much logistical work and co-ordination as it would have been if we chose China, the next best thing was to keep it Canadian, and walk the world's longest street, which was right in our own back yard – Yonge Street.

The potential held the same excitement as the Great Wall of China, unknown territory for the majority of the trip, the potential for the five of us to be together completing something that is in itself different from other charitable supporting causes in the fact that there would be not just one person traversing an insane distance, but five would take on the task.

Yonge Street itself holds impressive facts; it is the major arterial street in Toronto, Ontario and the northern residential areas of northern Ontario. Yonge Street holds the Guinness Book of Records as the longest street in the world at a total distance of 1,896km and has been deemed a national historical site. It was also the site of Canada's first subway line and separates the City of Toronto from east to west. Another interesting aspect of Yonge Street was that the regiment that I was serving with at the time, 'The Queens York Rangers', built a significant portion of the street in the later part of the seventeenth century. Back then the regiment was known as 'The Queens Rangers' and was led by John Graves Simcoe. Yonge Street is known as the road that leads to the Muskoka's for thousands of cottagers and summer enthusiasts, also everyone in the Toronto and surrounding areas have traversed at least part of the road at some point in their lives. What most people don't know is that number 1 Yonge Street is at the headways of Yonge and Queens Quay, and travels all the way to a small town called 'Rainy River', population 1000, which is 4 hours west of Thunder Bay and 3 hours east of Winnipeg. This would form our challenge and all five of my friends accepted the idea.

Then came the organizational component of the walk itself. We needed a name, and that was the first on the list. In Mom and Dad's living room sat, Andrew my brother, my good friend Jonathon Mishrigi and myself, going back and forth considering names to call our group before we presented in front of others. We were playing off the theme of five people completing the trek, names would be shouted out like '5 Alive' and then be critiqued for its close relations to the drink and the fact that it sounds fruity – '5 guys' was too generic and plain, '5 Amigos' was met with awkward looks. Then Andrew came out with 'Five with Drive'. It was marvelous! It held all the elements that we wanted, five people, and an adjective which described the grounds for our mission – inner drive to make a difference, to try something different and not be afraid to say that we are young, and we are not afraid to try and inspire others.

Second in our quest was to agree on what group we wanted to represent and what our message was for others to hear. Andrew had captured my attention when he became a big brother with York Region, and I was impressed with the mandate of the organization, which advocates a positive role model and adult friendship to children. Andrew inspired me to become a big brother in the program and I thought that bringing a message of friendship, a message of involvement, encouraging others to consider how they are spending their time and giving insight and inspiration for people to become involved in the lives of others - that would suffice as a worthy message.

Our primary goal was engaging people to reflect on how they can make a difference in the lives of others. I firmly believe that change happens when you personalize a cause, when you respond to something that touches your heart and when you donate your time and energy and become involved, that is when you will find that miracles do happen everyday. Money is neither a sufficient answer nor a solution when it comes to impacting someone's life. Don't get me wrong, as I mentioned earlier on, we all know that money is needed to conduct everyday living, and your money is especially needed to keep organizations across the country and organizations like the Five with Drive Foundation moving forward and starting new projects, there is no shortfall for the need of money. What I want to challenge you with is that if money is all that you give, you are shortchanging yourself and others.

Our money does not lend a helping hand, our money is not a shoulder to cry on or an ear that listens, our money doesn't laugh with those with disabilities and our money doesn't spare a tear when a mother receives an allotment of food to feed her family at Christmas time. YOU, have that ability to share in these moments if you choose – I chose Big Brothers and Big Sisters as the recipient of our efforts in our walk of Yonge Street because they existed when adults would identify and step up to the plate and volunteer their time with children who are lacking a role model in their life. To me, money was a by-product of our event and mission and not our focus. The tag line that I came up with prior to the walk was, 'Success is not measured in the dollars and cents but in the time we share with others and the difference we can make by investing our time'. There are so many causes out there and I am of the opinion that you don't need to pick the causes that I have advocated for or the causes that I believe in now. I am thankful when people have come up to me and told me that an event that I have been a part of has led them to an organization of their choice and they are becoming involved. I get excited when people get involved, that is where the difference is made and whether it's with a project of mine or a project of another, I want to be known as someone who challenges and inspires others to explore who they are and how they can make a difference in the lives of others, if only they personalize the change they want to make.

The walk that we undertook was 40 days long, 1,896 kilometers and our routine would start at the early hour of 3:30am in the morning, when we would arise, stumble about in the darkness of our rented U-haul trailer, find our clothes and shoes that we chose for the day and then would gather in front of our vehicle as our driver wondered why on earth he volunteered to drive for these five crazy people, who on average walked 50 kilometers a day. Before sunrise we would gather in a circle and say a prayer before we would start the day's journey. Besides the sunrises, laughs and people that we met on the walk, the last day was the most memorable. It was the completion of a commitment that was made by five individuals – and one dream.

Greg joined in the last 20 kilometers of the walk, mixed in with numerous people as we headed down Yonge Street in downtown Toronto with the road blocked off for our passage. Greg kept telling me that he loved me and that he was thankful the walk was for him. Greg tends to personalize things at times and had it in his mind that I planned the walk all around him – I never corrected his thoughts, rather added a soft response "and for kids that don't have positive role models as well".

Greg was walking with my Dad that day as we headed to Yonge Street's end, sweat beading off, short legs moving in double time to keep up with the crowd. I was proud that my friend made the last leg with us. Around 3 kilometers from the finish, we excused the multitude that had followed us to go ahead so we could finish this journey as the five who started it 40 days prior.

With arms interlocked, we walked the last steps of our journey and were embraced by our friends, family and supporters. I can recall my teammates being embraced by their loved ones – tears freely rolling and a feeling of elation that our mission was accomplished. At our ceremony each of the members were given the opportunity to share their thoughts on the journey. The truth was told about our fun, our difficulties and leadership. When it was my turn to speak – I shared briefly on my personal account of the trip and chose to speak on the reason why we undertook such an endeavor. That night I spoke with conviction and passion and I spoke on behalf of the children that we were seeking to help. Those gathered around at our homecoming were more interested in our 'stories' and less concerned about our motivation that fueled us – I just wanted to ensure that the audience received insight into the need for mentoring our young minds.

I missed Greg while I was away at university. Since the walk took half of my summer that year I didn't have that much time to hang out with my buddy. Greg and I were at the calling phase of our friendship, where finally he was calling me to hang out, whereas before, it was mostly me calling and asking his parents if I could take Greg out. As I started my third year of university I wished I had more time to answer the phone calls from Greg and know that in 5 minutes I could pick him up and go for an ice cappuccino.

At this point I had known Greg for 7 years and wanted to let the rest of his family know how much his friendship had meant to me. I planned for an evening where I would treat the O'Brien's for dinner and express to them how their son had impacted my life. The thought choked me up and the plan never came to fruition but for whatever reason I felt the need to let the O'Brien's know that their disabled son, to me, was a very close friend. I desperately wanted to let Jenny know the impression that Greg had made on my heart and that he had taught me so much about friendship and love. She was raising an amazing son and I felt she should know that, above all else, in my heart I saw Greg as Greg and not as a boy with a disability and that I accepted Greg for who he was and I considered him a friend above all else. Yet, when it came time to make the call I was nervous. I waited until my roommates were gone and the house quiet, I paced back and forth in the kitchen for what seemed like an eternity. I had such a difficult time before I made that call because when you share your feelings with someone you become vulnerable and that is how I felt. When I finally dialed the numbers and the phone rang, Jenny picked up on the other end and as I began to share my feelings, tears welled up as I told her that at first it was a job for me but I could never have foreseen what would become of Greg's and my path's crossing.

A friend of mine who worked at the Salvation Army Church in Markham as a youth pastor was going through a position transition within the church and was moving into the department of family services. When he told me about the move, my immediate thoughts turned to the youth group that he led and what would happen to the small gathering? For whatever reason, God put it on my heart to lead the small group that met every Tuesday night in Markham. I had classes on Tuesday until 4pm and it was a two-hour drive back to Markham from Guelph, regardless of the time it took to travel and the fact that I had class Wednesday morning I was excited to teach and share with this group. With no previous experience leading youth groups I decided that I wanted to develop leaders through the seminars that I would be preparing. The plan was to engage the kids on relevant issues and bring in the Bible's responses to the challenges in their life!

Interaction was the key to what I wanted to accomplish with the group. I was seeking to establish a teach the teacher environment were the kids would use their experiences that they were going through and cross reference biblical scripture to discuss solutions to their problems. My roommates thought I was nuts for taking on this project, the travel time alone was something that turned them off but I saw it as more of an opportunity than anything else. Not only would I be engaging in teaching, something that I thoroughly enjoyed doing, travelling back to Markham every Tuesday gave me the opportunity to see Greg as well. I called Jenny and told her about my new undertaking and asked if I could pick up Greg on the way and bring him to the youth group gatherings. With no hesitation at all Jenny said 'yes', and subsequently resolved the problem of not seeing Greg as frequently as I wanted. Greg was definitely down with the arrangements and without fail would be waiting outside his house every Tuesday when

I went to pick him up. As I told you before, Greg has this amazing fascination with music and as I would turn onto his street, there Greg would be, head phones on, 'CD player' in hand singing whatever song was playing. Greg would jump into Frank, (my truck) say 'hi', and then want me to put on his CD into the player where he would continue singing. It was almost like routine, when the music was too loud for me I would turn it down. I wished at times that I could turn Greg down but that never happened and I just grew fond of his energy to sing.

Regarding the youth group, I had asked Andrew to come along to mostly keep Greg company and more importantly because I knew that I could count on his insight and presence and his support. I also called upon a former football player of mine to hang out and be exposed to a more positive environment and help with the technological aspects of the seminars. Miles Krauter played defensive tackle for me and he was entering his final year at my former high school and while volunteering that Christmas with my family at the food bank he had expressed to me that he was getting into trouble with his friends and making wrong decisions in life. When I met Miles he was in grade 9 and showed up to his first football practice asking, "Sir, do you think I'll be ok playing football?" I didn't see any reason why he wouldn't be, so I responded, "of course, you'll be fine".

Miles told me that he was worried because he only had one kidney – "A big one at that, though", were his reassuring words but one kidney nonetheless. Miles would go on to become the captain of the team when I left football and would hold a spot in my heart as a hard working young man. Naturally, when he shared with me that he was having trouble I was concerned and wanted to help in any way I could – asking him to be a part of the youth group was the first thought I had when presented with the opportunity to lead.

The next person that I had asked to come along for the journey was my buddy Marcel Destine. Marcel is a great, happy go lucky kind of guy. Marcel was Andrew's age and played football and rugby with both Andrew and me – and he had an older brother that I grew up with throughout high school that I knew very well and had worked with at day camp – he was the one that helped me change my first diaper! When Marcel would connect with my brother, the two stirred a continuous storm of laughter and enjoyable moments. Marcel had a brother who had at the time recently perished. His younger brother was living with numerous physical and intellectual disabilities and had been best friends with Greg. Marcel was having a difficult time with different things in life and in the hopes to be the best friend that I could be to him, I asked him to join in our group as a solution.

These four guys didn't know it but they formed my support group. I treated all of these guys like my younger brothers and knowing that they were in need made it all the more worthwhile driving two hours to be with them and the other youth.

I enjoyed presenting my ideas to the group, I probably put more time into preparing messages than I did school at the time. This was my way of establishing the status rev for my life, I didn't want to become a robot in university, secluded from the outside world and living in a bubble, this youth group was a way to escape student life and be around the people that meant a lot to me. I would like to think that the messages I prepared were received well, the group never seemed to be overly disinterested so I took that as a sign that I was doing somewhat of a good job. The group participated in open discussion and wasn't afraid of asking questions and shared their insight. Any teacher would love for their classes to be that involved.

The youth group usually ran from 7pm to around 8:30pm, and I would see the kids out waiting for their parents in the front of the church, sometimes I would get held up with a chatty parent asking how things went, that they appreciated what I was doing because they felt that if I wasn't, their kids would have had to go to another youth group... blah,blah,blah. Not to be insensitive, but I knew that Marcel, Andrew, Miles and Greg were having fun either playing basketball in the gym or playing video games and that is where I wanted to be more than being an adult talking about adult things with adults!

Observation skills are a special skill of mine and I know when someone I am speaking with becomes un-interested or mentally taken to another spot and I struggled trying not to overly show my itching to join my friends when I was being stalled by parents – I just hope that they didn't hold it against me!

As I was politely pushing people out the door, in the background coming from the sanctuary I could hear a familiar song being played over the entertainment system. I left the conversation that someone was trying to engage me with and walked towards the sanctuary.

The sanctuary could seat around 150 people, and was enclosed with glass sliding doors that were usually closed. On a side note, Andrew was the janitor that year at the church as a part-time gig, and his number one demise was when handprints would appear on the glass doors and occasionally when I helped him, that was mine as well!

I halted just short of the glass door and peered in – the music was pumping 'Backstreet Boys' and the boys were all on the small stage of the church, Greg had a microphone, Miles was on the drums, Andrew and Marcel were jumping from pew to pew – back to the stage and singing the parts that they knew as loud as they could! It wasn't pretty nor did it sound good at all but they were having fun and I didn't want to spoil it. I desperately wanted to join them but I thought my presence might deter their enthusiasm or bring the 'responsible older brother' complex into the fun. As the first song came to an end, Greg quickly yelled through the microphone for me to join the ad-hoc band and without missing a step I was through the door and took a position on the piano. The next song was already in the queue and the five of us just went all out...no holding back, without a care in the world and not afraid to express ourselves amongst each other. Greg was centre stage, mic in hand and singing with poise and emotion as if he was in front of a crowd of a thousand.

Andrew and Marcel, one foot on pew benches the other on the back rest, seriating a woman if there were to be one there. Miles had moved from the drum set and was crawling over the stage clutching his fist with the emotion that the song carried. I was doing a Stevie Wonder on the piano – not able to play the piano, I hit the keys and that day it just sounded in sync with everything else that was going on. We put so much energy into that song that by the end of it we were exhausted and light headed from our all-star effort.

As we all sat around recovering from the song, I was overwhelmed with thoughts about what had just transpired. People knew that I was a friend with Greg and that I would bring him to various places with me and include Greg in activities that I engaged with as much as I could. But that night, I witnessed a group of my friends fully accept Greg and not in that awkward way most of my friends had of not knowing how to talk to Greg and resorting to a child like approach partly because they felt that people with exceptionalities had the mind of children and that is how they thought you talk to them. That night though, Marcel, Andrew and Miles without knowing it, became vulnerable and allowed themselves to join Greg in the fun of the moment. For me the best part was that it all started without me, as I was watching from the sanctuary, I had a smile on my face as I saw the connection between the boys. No one was afraid to express themselves and no one was afraid to dream with Greg. You don't forget moments like that and Greg truly received three other friends that night who accepted him for who he was and not the label that was associated to him.

As I drove Greg home that night he was raving about the fun that he had. His excitement was contagious "Did you see me on stage, Daniel?" Greg is one of the only people other than Mom to call me Daniel. "Of course I did, I was there with you", I responded. Greg went on about how good he was and how he loved the fact that the rest of us joined him. Greg was on such a high that we drove around the block a couple of times so he could finish listening to the 'Backstreet Boys' playing through Frank's poorly made stereo system. Frank must have had a loose wire somewhere because every time we drove over a bump or railway tracks, the CD would skip and Greg would quickly say, "Aw, Daniel", as if it was my fault! Most times I would bring a haymaker to the dashboard and the CD would jump back into the track it was playing. Everytime that I would bring Greg home I would walk him to the door, without fail and if I ever forgot Greg would state, "Well aren't you going to walk me"? To this day, I can't say that I've just dropped Greg off at his house and drove off, I have walked the steps leading to the front door and watched him sound off without fail, regardless of the time of day or night, as loud as he could that "I am HOME"! I'd laugh and tell him that he'd wake up the neighbors yelling like that but I wasn't going to tell him to stop either, it was what he did and who was I to try and change it. Greg had expressed to me that he couldn't wait until next Tuesday when we got to hang out again and asked if he could sing after the youth group was done.

Before class on Wednesday I had a shift at the library – usually I was tired as I pushed my cart with books that needed to be shelved. I always wanted to work at a library, subsequently my request that year was for clothes that would make me look like a librarian...but those never came.

The library was great, the guys on the rugby team I played on, mocked me for the venture I undertook and when my friends back in Markham found out they had a great laugh on my behalf. No matter how funny it was for others to hear that I worked at the library, they would inevitably stop laughing when good looking girls would approach me to ask for help! I cannot answer the question as to why I took the job but it definitely had its perks besides the paycheck.

For a librarian I was quite loud, and was known for running down the aisles with my cart, gathering speed and then jumping on for the ride. Students I'm sure didn't know what to make of it and my supervisor who, on numerous occasions warned me not to continue the antics, admitted that when she started at the library 20 years earlier... she did the same thing. The next morning after band practice, while I was in the middle of my work routine, in the middle of my shift, I got a phone call from Greg.

"Daniel, what do you think about starting a band" – Greg could hardly hold back his enthusiasm.

"Sounds good buddy but how about we talk later, I'm at the library working". Greg was one of those people that would laugh when he heard I worked at the library and would chuckle if I made mention about it. "But, Daniel, I think it's a good idea, I want to be in a band", Greg continued. "Alright buddy, I'll see what I can do but I have to go back to work, we'll talk later". "Ok, I'll call you tonight" Greg ended. And I hung up. Greg called me that afternoon, still excited and told me that he was printing off lyrics for the Tuesday coming up.

Sure enough, after I summed up the youth group that following Tuesday, Greg opened up a folder and handed Marcel, Andrew, Miles and I a sheet with printed out lyrics. I was impressed, Greg had finally found something that he was passionate about and took the initiative to prep lyrics. He was serious and the guys were all taken back. It was a painful first practice, all of us were tone deaf and we struggled with singing to the Backstreet Boys and couldn't find the beat.

I don't know how Greg does it but when he shares something that he wants to do with me and if it's in my power, like I said before, I will try to make it come true for him. After practice that night, Greg told me that he thought it would be cool to perform on stage and be a band! That was enough for me; one thing that I have learned over the years is this; when your heart speaks...take good notes! I told Greg to pack up his stuff and head to the truck. I stalled the boys and told them what I was thinking.

"Guys, Greg's pretty serious and I've never seen him having so much fun before, all he wants is for us to start a band together and I think it's a pretty decent idea. We can practice every Tuesday night after youth group and I'll find us a place to play". It sounded innocent enough and since the guys were having fun already they all agreed. The only exception was that we had to sing other songs besides 'Backstreet Boys'.

It wasn't hard to find a place to play, Greg started spreading the word that we were a band quite fast and in a heartbeat his assistant at school found us a location to play. Mai Lin Bozian was Greg's assistant at Brother Andre for eight years and an amateur photographer. When she found out, it was an immediate phone call and the offer to come and take pictures of us at one of our practices. The stage that was offered to us was at Brother Andre, which was Andrew, Marcel and my former high school and for Miles and Greg their current school. We were to be an act on what the school dubbed 'B.A Day'. B.A. day was a day that the school held different activities for the students and music provided by school bands and we were going to be one of those bands. Truthfully, I skipped B.A. days when I was in school and now I was going to be singing in one of the performances.

The weeks leading up to Greg's big day were filled with excitement. Greg would call me while I was at school and use up my phone minutes sharing his enthusiasm, anxiety and everything else. Greg would discuss how he thought Andrew was tone deaf, Marcel needed a haircut and Miles needed to practice more. Greg never critiqued me; rather he would copiously compliment my singing and style. Greg would call me, "Big Sexy" and I have no idea where he got that nickname but it stuck! I never minded when Greg would call, when I am away from Greg, as I was in university and as I am now writing this book, I try to be there to answer his calls and hear about what's on his mind.

Practices had come a long way from when we had started. There was no argument when we had to decide on a name to call our little group of singers and 'Greg and the Boys' was the name we settled on. Since it was Greg's dream to be in a band and perform what better-suited name than that!

Just like any amateur band we needed an outfit for the stage. Mom had purchased 5 white T-shirts and iron on letters to showcase the name we chose. I came home from working with the military one weekend and saw Mom working on the shirts that we would wear for our first concert. Mom had left the front of the shirts blank and the back of the shirts read in big blue lettering, "Greg and the Boys". It was official.

The day of the concert we donned our white shirt and blue jeans, Marcel had gotten a haircut, Andrew worked on his tone, and Miles had learned his lyrics. I was 24 years old at the time of our first concert and as our group was waiting to go on stage; my thoughts were filled with my days at high school. The kids that had formed around the bandstand and the crowds looked much younger than what I thought I looked like when I was their age. The conversations that I had overheard were filled with immature banter or hot gossip about boys and girls none of which I knew. I hoped that I didn't sound so immature when I was at their age. I thought of how all those watching would respond to our performance. Most of the students knew Greg and Miles who both had their own crowd of friends in attendance, some of the football players that I had coached were scattered throughout the crowd, some of my old teachers were looking on in anticipation and I became nervous. Greg was beside himself!

I had received so many phone calls with Greg yelling into the phone, "OH MY GOD, DANIEL, I'm so excited...! I can't wait". This was the norm for Greg's phone calls. Yet, on the day of the concert he was frozen with anxiety and shyness. All the boys were putting in so much support for Greg, telling him that 'it will be fine...you don't have to worry', but Greg wasn't hearing anything of it. The effort that we were lending to Greg kept us from thinking about our own stress in the moments leading up to our first ever performance. With all the time dedicated to practice, with the hard work of learning 'Backstreet Boys' music, Greg did not want to go on stage. We had come so far and had more fun than I personally had in years and now the reason why we called ourselves 'Greg and the Boys' was too afraid to perform!

I took Greg aside, away from the crowd and had a heart to heart with the little man; "Greg, no matter what happens out there, if we perform or if we don't, I am so proud of you! The Boys and I have had so much fun and we want you to know that this is for you, and if you decide that you don't want to sing…that's fine with us!" My hand was on Greg's warm damp back, Greg was so nervous that he was sweating profusely. I could see the anxiety in his eyes and he kept shaking his head back and forth. My friend had come so far and I couldn't help but think how proud I was of him. "You know, I'll be there right beside you the whole time and I think that it would be pretty cool if you sang, this is what you've talked about for the past 4 months and how awesome would it be to have your dream come true?" These were my last words to Greg, I had nothing left, I told him how I felt and the rest was up to him – that's when Greg said with much hesitation , "Dan, I don't want people to see me…and I need my lyrics!" 'Well, I'll tell you what, how about you wear my sunglasses – you can see out but people can't see in, and if you really want…although I don't agree with it, because you know the songs better than any one of us, you can sing with your lyrics". "Can I wear my Toronto Maple Leafs hat?" Greg responded, and with that I knew that our lead singer was back! "You know Greg…we couldn't do this without you…you are our lead singer!" Greg cracked a smile and gave me a big hug, his shirt was now completely soaked as I wrapped my arms around him.

The stage could hardly fit all five of us on it – in our act we incorporated a couple of songs from the Temptations and The Supremes. The technical aspect to our perform- ance wasn't tough at all, we just sang to a CD that played. Before we started, Greg was receiving cheers from his fel- low students who also had exceptionalities which helped lift his spirits. Greg had my sunglasses on, his hat on back- wards and lyrics in his hand as we walked on stage. I voiced a little commentary about the story of Greg and the Boys, highlighting the fun that we have had and the dream that Greg had shared with me and now it is about to become a reality.

And just like that, our first concert began! Greg took his spot in the middle of the group, I promised to stand beside him and he had his lyrics in front of his face... We all tried to tell him that no lead singers have lyrics when they perform but he would have nothing to hear of it. At the end of it we were just happy that Greg was on stage and was singing.

Unlike the band that was on before us, we had the crowd rocking right off the get go! With a mix of well known old school songs and the ever famous 'Backstreet Boys' it didn't take long before we had people dancing. Our biggest support came from the students with exceptionalities that gave all they had, no holding back and their energy was contagious. Their assistants joined in the fun, followed by students that weren't afraid to express themselves.

When we started singing all the nervousness left my body. The boys were on their game and regardless of how we sounded we put everything we had into that performance to make it the most memorable for Greg. Above all else we wanted to show people that it didn't matter how good you were, anyone could obtain their dreams with hard work, commitment and more importantly by having fun throughout the journey!

Greg never would let the lyrics down and kept his face covered for the entire act. Greg didn't want Jenny his mother at the concert because he was afraid that he would cry if he saw her. She was at the back of the gathered crowd out of sight, but I'm sure that she was the proudest mother on earth while she saw her son, defying the disability he was born with and living his dream. Thank you God for allowing me to be a part of such a precious moment as the first time I shared a stage with Greg O'Brien.

On our last song for our performance we lined-up to sing 'Incomplete' by the 'Backstreet Boys', Greg started an uncontrollable cry. It broke my heart to see my friend in such a state. The tears were rolling underneath his sunglasses, and the shaking that starts when you are crying hard had started and I knew that Greg would not be able to sing the last song with us. I placed my arm around his shoulders, his shirt wetter than ever and the vibrations of his shaking felt by my supportive arm. I sang Greg's lines that song, and was holding back the tears myself. A friend of mine had once told me that, 'What soap is for the body, tears are for the soul'

Ironically enough, I never fully understood the meaning of that parable, until I saw Greg crying on stage for our last song. I don't know why Greg was crying and I may never know, but those tears reflected something powerful going on in Greg's heart when we started singing that song. And more than anyone else there that day, that song touched a note in Greg and we just let him soak it all up! As a matter of fact, that would be the first and only time that Greg would cry during a song in the multitude of performances that we would go on to host.

For the weeks and months to follow, Greg would picturesquely replay his first concert. Greg was in heaven from that day on; from his phone calls to the ice caps that we shared at Tim Horton's, Greg re-lived the precious moments on stage and thanked the Boys for helping him live his dream.

I believe that at the time we formed 'Greg and the Boys' our focal point was that one concert for Greg to experience. In the aftermath of that concert, we found ourselves wanting to continue practicing the fun and excitement after youth group couldn't just stop like that. We toned down the amount that we practiced but kept the band alive. Our practice platform had moved from the church sanctuary to our vehicles parked at Greg's favorite place to go, the Tim Horton's parking lot at 16th Ave and Markham Rd. Greg loved performing and more than anything else in the world wanted one more performance as Greg and the Boys.

Third Year University came quicker than I thought it would. I struggled with being older than the majority of the student population. I took a spot on the rugby team for another season, took another round of work at the school library, kept busy with the military reserves and decided to stay on with the youth group that I had led the year previous. Remarkably I found time for school – I've never made the Dean's list but I never failed a class either.

The days leading to the start of my last year, Greg on one of our trips to Tim Horton's told me how cool it would be if he could sing in a concert once more and that he was serious. A smile lit my face from ear to ear, I simply asked if he was sure that is what he wanted, and with all the confidence in the world, Greg's answer was 'Yes'.

Since I was confined to school most days during the week, I decided that organizing a concert at the university was our best bet, knowing that I would return to Markham once a week for practices to enable the band to stay connected and provide an opportunity to put the pieces of the puzzle together for the concert in Guelph. There was only one problem, I had never organized a concert before and I hadn't the faintest clue where to start!

CHAPTER THIRTEEN

GREG AND THE BOYS

I think it's neat that people with all abilities and disabilities have something to offer this world.

- Andrew Rossi

Fear doesn't keep me from moving forward. When I led my friends down Yonge Street, I asked them to write their thoughts on paper about the walk, what excited them, what scared them, how they thought this was beneficial in supporting mentoring for children and the most memorable quote that I would read was from my brother, Andrew;

'It's not fear that holds us back from living our dreams, it's the thought of fear that keeps us from moving forward'.

(Andrew Rossi)

Man that's powerful! I wasn't afraid to involve myself with organizing a concert when I had no idea where or how to start. I was satisfied that my friend Greg O'Brien had shown me so much through friendship and had gotten me to do things that I'd never imagined, so I felt that organizing a concert, if that was what he truly wanted, would be a gift of gratitude.

I formed a committee – which meant that I just asked people who I thought would be beneficial to the end goal, passionate and dedicated. It turned out that no one in the group that I had gathered had any experience with organizing concerts. My next focus was on leading with confidence and not allowing people to feel defeated before we started. I held the view that if you're confident enough chances are people generally won't challenge you or break down your dreams with pessimism or fear of failure. I've met many a person who has disqualified the ideas that I have run with. Most of my pursuits have led to nowhere but it was the journey that built my character and I was mature enough to know that failure is only failure by the one who perceives it to be. I treated failure as a learning experience. Organizing a concert would be no different than walking the world's longest street; you express your end goal to your team and start working towards the results. My end goal was to have my friend experience a true concert – on a stage, in front of a large crowd were Greg and the Boys would be the main act.

I started organizing the concert in October, with a show date of February 2nd, we had a little less than four months to put the show on. I separated the team with different tasks, and formed what I deemed manageable due dates. The team I had was great and never missed a meeting – they adopted the cause that I tagged to the concert and that was built around Greg living his dream – Focusing on the 'Ability' instead of 'Dis-Ability', with people living with exceptionalities. What I learnt off the bat was that not everyone is as passionate as I am at times. I don't expect everyone that I have worked with on projects that have touched my heart to be full throttle into making it happen. I mean it would be nice if we all put passion to good use and make the changes we want, but that is not always the case. We are all full of ideas, no doubt and our ears have burned with fantastic, creative works, whether they be our own, or from a friend. On a side note, we have also heard some not so good ideas. Nonetheless, ideas good or bad stay in that state until you insert some passion behind it to make it mobile. I think that those in my team really liked the idea that I was organizing a concert for my friend who had a disability and chances were that Greg on his own accord could not organize such an event but that is why God introduced him to me.

Mom taught me to listen to others and that has made me intuitive and I catch the little things that people say and remember them, big or small and if I could make their dream come true for them I will try.

From the time that it was decided to host another concert for my little friend, the local television channel caught wind of what Greg and the Boys were all about. This was fantastic, not only did they want to interview Greg; they were also asking if we would sing two songs on live television to help promote our upcoming concert. Greg did not have the slightest concern of missing school for the day when we were asked to come into the studio for our first ever television performance. The boys were all in for the experience and Andrew had gone out to Wal-Mart to purchase five identical dress shirts for our debut.

Like little kids in a candy store is the only way to explain what we were like when we arrived at the studio, giggling and joking around as if this was more natural to us than it really was. Greg was a tad nervous and made it clear that he wanted me to sit beside him during the interview in the event that he got stuck answering a question – the whole time I was telling him that he had nothing to worry about! To settle Greg's nerves – Marcel, Andrew and Miles started play fighting in the 'green' room that we were waiting in before going out to record the two songs that we selected. For as long as I can remember Greg loves WWF wrestling and keeps the rest of us up-to-date as to who's who, and when the biggest fights are taking place. When the boys would wrestle, Greg would cheer them on and quickly forget what was causing him to be nervous. At some point one of the boys would pull Greg into the mix, or hold Miles and it was always Miles that was pinned to the ground so Greg could belly flop on him. The second that the tables would turn and someone would playfully hold Greg, he would yell his distress call, "Daniel…. help me!!!" It was always said with a smile. I pulled the big brother card and watched, as the boys would wrestle on the ground, the day of our first T.V performance was no different.

I watched in amusement as the Boys allowed themselves to become vulnerable (something that I learnt awhile ago) and role-play to make Greg feel at ease. The stir that they were causing caught the attention of a late 60-year-old stage manager who rushed into the Green room to see what all the commotion was. The manager had these extremely large glasses that covered her face, a haircut that made her hair look more like an umbrella than anything else and had no sense of humor at all! She quickly retorted her frustration at our excited bunch and as the boys picked themselves off the ground I found it more amusing that they were being reprimanded for being themselves.

'Ain't No Mountain High Enough', a song from Marvin Gaye a duet that Greg and I sing was the first song that we were to perform, followed by 'Quit playing games with my Heart' by the Backstreet Boys – and we hit both songs on tone and did not miss a beat!

After our performance, Greg and I took a seat on a big comfy sofa for the interview. The host was a beautiful woman that was making Greg blush before we started the interview and before she started the interview Greg pulled me close, so he could whisper 'Can you tell I'm blushing', in my ear. Greg did well answering all the questions that were directed towards him and I filled in the advertising plugs for our concert and where to purchase tickets. The day was a success and it started the momentum that the band and I needed to put all we had into this concert.

No one on the committee for the concert had any issues with the roles that they accepted but when push came to shove and due dates came and went, I realized that passion is contagious but passion does not always result in hard work. Hard work is in a class of its own. The other things that I wasn't as sensitive as I should have been on were that all my team members were students and with that meant student life. It was hard for me to accept that not all students were like me, with a million and one things on the go and still able to maintain a B average in school. Most students I knew found it difficult to balance a full time course load, perhaps a part-time job and/or a sport, not to mention, the much praised social life as well. I am of the heart that if people care about something that they would simply do it! So when the two girls that were in charge of creating the tickets and having them printed before the Christmas break didn't get them done, I wasn't upset, I just made a couple of phone calls, made a quick design and had them printed you could say, behind their backs. Granted they were upset but they also were over the dead line by two weeks and had nothing to show for their work. Hosting a concert for Greg meant the world to me and there was no time to waste and I couldn't afford to standby as things were pending to be completed. Yes, perfectionism does run through my veins but could you blame me, I was working for my friend and why shouldn't it be perfect☺

Jenny allowed Greg to spend the night before the concert at my house in Guelph with the boys. Next to the concert, spending a night with the boys was Greg's ultimate source of entertainment.

My room was on the first floor of the house, a family room converted into a bedroom and I would hear the music blasting from their car a block away and knew that they had arrived. When the boys stepped into the house it would have been to the equivalent of a hurricane registering a 5.0 on the Richter scale. Health went right through the window as pizzas were ordered, cans of coke were drunk and my room was in a mess that made me cringe. The night before the concert was filled with laughter, practice and before bed a movie that has since left my memory.

The end was near, I awoke early to a group of half naked men, snoring and clothes scattered all over the floor and a phone call that the group of guys I had hired to run the technical realms of the concert were sick and couldn't attend. I went into a panic. I called every music store in town and in the next town over and not a single store could spare two guys to set up all the tech equipment. To boot, I called the friend in charge of picking up all the sound equipment from a music store in Cambridge which was one hour away and was told that he went to the gym for a work out. The problem was that the equipment needed to be picked up by eleven o'clock and the time was 9am. I wasn't going to count on my friend to workout, shower and drive an hour to Cambridge and make it on time. I was deflated. It seemed that in half an hour my world and efforts to make Greg's dream come true entered an unsalvageable tailspin. I jumped in my truck and left for Cambridge on a prayer. On the drive over all I could think about was how I wanted to be there with Greg walking around campus, hanging out before his big day and now I was picking up after others and trying desperately to find a technician to ensure the concert went on. I called Andrew from the road and told him to take the guys around and have fun, since I was busy with last minute details I told him to meet me at the concert hall for sound check by 4pm. That gave me 5 hours to find a technician.

Without a clue in the world, I said a prayer, I asked God that he forgive me for the way I treated those that had helped organize the concert and that He provide a person to perform all the technical aspects that we needed for the night to be a success. Not a couple of minutes had passed when I received a call from one of the many contacts that I had made through the phone book asking for help. I answered the phone and must have sounded stressed because the reply to my hello was "you alright man"? I felt stupid for my harsh greeting. "Are you Dan Rossi", the voice was quick to ask. "Yes, that's me, and who may I ask am I speaking with?" The voice was calm and cool, I immediately thought of the voice of the sea turtles from the movie *Finding Nemo.*

"Ya, I'm the guy who's going to come and work the show tonight for you. A buddy of mine called me telling me how you need someone desperately and I cleared my schedule tonight to help you guys out, I think what you guys are doing is great and I don't mind being a part of this." He then told me his name, and said he was looking forward to helping out. I was elated!!! A big "Thank you Lord", followed that phone call. Not only did I get a tech, this guy had worked on sets for 'Nickleback' for many years.

When I pulled up to the theater hall with all the equipment to be unloaded my friend who originally had that responsibility met me. He pulled me aside and told me how he felt unappreciated and that I just went behind his back and didn't trust him to get the task done.

"You're right, I totally did. I was expecting a bit more responsibility and thought it pretty selfish of you to go for a work out and jeopardize not making it on time for the pick-up of the equipment and when I didn't hear back from you I did it myself." When you speak the truth, leave immediately afterwards. That friendship was never lost but it was never the same after that day either.

With all the scrambling, time flew and sound check came and went. Our tech guy was unbelievable, for a one-man operation he had everything and everyone wired up to meet his or her group and individual needs. There were three other bands playing with us that night and back stage was a zoo of instruments, cords, stage props and people. The place was humming and I needed a break. This was crazy; I underestimated how much work went into a concert and thought that I would have been able to spend time with the band and Greg during the day, soaking in the experience. With 20 minutes until show time I found myself on the top balcony looking down on the stage. It was hard for me to visualize the 435 empty seats that awaited their patrons for the evening entertainment. I saw people finally taking interest in the concert and running back and forth putting the final touches together before the show. I wanted to relish the moment that I was in, I watched as Andrew sat beside Greg in the front row, and how I wanted to be there. I thought of how the two had become friends, through me by default, but truly friends now. Over the months that I was away at university Greg would call Andrew and vice versa and they went for ice caps. They were friends and that made me happy. Greg was starting to have friends that weren't other children with disabilities, friends who treated him like a person and I couldn't hold back the tears of happiness. It was short-lived, however, because my tears were interrupted by someone who found me to ask a question but at least I had a few quiet moments to take it all in.

All the bands gathered in the basement of the concert hall, and the idea of linking arms to form a solid intertwined circle enthralled me as a good idea to start an event. Linking symbolic gestures such as forming a circle, thanking all those involved with the event and those that were performing, and saying a prayer was my idea of an appropriate common ground to stand on before we started. The story of Greg's dream was shared in that circle and the gleam in everyone's eyes confirmed that the magic of Greg's first concert was about to happen. After the break everyone started moving towards their respected spots, I noticed my friend had isolated himself in the corner of a small room. "Dan, I don't think I can do this", Greg admitted. "Brother of course you can, and the boys will be there with you the whole time...right by your side". I can't imagine how Greg felt that night; it took a while to bring him up from the basement of the concert hall to the stage to watch the first band as they performed.

Greg and the Boys, were the closing band and we thought that it would give Greg time to warm up and get used to the environment before we took the stage. The boys were great with their support and none of us wanted to push Greg past his comfort zone.

"Daniel" – It gets me every time when Greg uses my full name. "How bout I sing from off stage, and you guys sing on the stage....How bout that?" Greg, at this point, was sitting on a chair and the Master of Ceremonies had started with his pre-amble before he introduced our band. "I don't know Dan...I just don't" and with those words Greg started to cry. I was crouched down in front of him, his head was down and I could see the tears falling from his cheeks to his pants. The boys were set behind the closed curtain...waiting.

My heart broke – I couldn't hold back the tears either, all the running around, all the craziness, all the work seemed futile at that moment. The hard work was for Greg to live his dream and enjoy the whole experience; I wish I had more time with him during the day to be with him and the boys. We had been down this road before when we sang at Greg's school. In practice Greg would sing and act without any fear as though he were in front of a crowd of a thousand. The best part of being in *Greg and the Boys* was the practices – to quantify the amount of fun we had during our sessions is extremely hard to explain. The emotion and energy that went into our practices was epic and suffice to say, I can't imagine many other people in this world having as much innocent fun as the members in *Greg and the Boys* have had.

I found myself repeating my words to Greg that night before the curtains were set to open.

"Greg, no matter what you choose to do...if you stay here, or come out on stage, I'm proud of you. I have had so much fun being in this band and have laughed so hard until my stomach hurts and I'm crying. That has made this journey so memorable to me and the Boys, this is just another practice for us out there."

All four of us had our sunglasses on, to support Greg; we were wearing the shirts Andrew picked up for our television performance and blue jeans. I took my spot next to Miles and awaited the Master of Ceremonies to conclude his introduction and for the curtain to open. All of the boys must have been focused on the curtain opening because we didn't hear Greg scamper to the back right hand corner of the stage and grab a mic – but when he said that he was ready and that, "I'm going to stand here and sing and not in front", we all instantly had a smile on our faces as the music started for our opening song! The crowd was moving with every song we sang. Loads of supporters had travelled the two-hour trek from Markham, Ontario to Guelph that night to watch Greg live his dream. There were signs held up by fans and people with exceptionalities dancing at front stage and in the crowds. The atmosphere was electric and we held nothing back! At one point I remember my cheeks hurting from smiling so much and wondered if it was affecting my singing skills!

When you're on stage, time goes by so fast and we were approaching our last song quicker than we expected. The story of *Greg and the Boys* was shared with the crowd – the testimony that was shared reflected friendship and how we all have something special to offer this world because of our 'ability', rather than our 'disability'. Wet eyes were found throughout the audience as I opened my heart and shared about the friendship that

had and was changing my life. After the words were spoken, I retreated behind the curtain for our last song of the
night, and Greg by now was closer to the front and said, "I
didn't know you felt that way about me bro"! I was glad
to see that he wasn't as nervous and that he was enjoying
this experience. "You bet buddy – meant every word of
it". And with that we would end our first concert in a wave
of cheers and hollering!

After the concert, people were lining up for pictures
of our band and congratulating Greg. It was the closest
thing to feeling like a star for the boys as we signed some
autographs and joined in the pictures, however, it was
short lived since we were a part of the clean up party.
I'm sure when the infamous band U2 puts on a show they
don't have to tear down the set afterwards and I imagine
that they are escorted off the stage to a quiet room to
relax and wind down. That would had been nice if we
had that treatment but it was a luxury that we couldn't
afford. We left Greg to enjoy the surrounding crowd and
his family who are so great at supporting him and we took
off our dress shirts and started the clean up.

CHAPTER FOURTEEN

THE FIVE WITH DRIVE FOUNDATION

Never doubt that a small group of thoughtful committed citizens can change the world indeed.
It's the only thing that ever has.

- Margaret Mead

Greg joined the five of us as we approached our final steps from Halifax to Markham

'Let us not love in word and talk, but in action and in truth'

(1 John 3:18)

Digressing a little, at the age of 15, I had a vision of climbing the stairs of the CN Tower in an effort to raise money for the children's hospital in Toronto. The first course of action I took was gathering pledge forms at the high school I attended to find out how many people would be interested. It only took one lunch hour or so for 150 names with contact information to appear on the sheets, I was impressed.

Step number two was contacting the President of the CN Tower and to my astonishment that was rather easy and painless. After placing my call I received a phone call back two days later and enjoyed a 45-minute conversation with the man in charge of the Tower's operations. The idea was welcomed and encouraged and I thought that this was a walk in the park. The President was patient with my laborious questioning and offered some much welcomed advice.

Step three; I arranged a meeting with the head of Sick Kids Hospital in Toronto, which took weeks for an opening to meet with them due to the sheer volume of meetings and bookings the position demanded. Dad drove me downtown for the meeting, and walked up the flight of stairs to the department that housed the administrators and charitable employees the hospital counts on for year round support. I walked with an air of confidence; my game plan was to share my idea that I had and truthfully thought that it would be received with appreciation and why not? Essentially, the hospital would be the recipient of my philanthropic endeavor. Then I would show the director the pledge forms with all the people who would commit to the challenge being proposed and then wait for the smile and vote of confidence.

I got the smile all right but the vote of confidence was more like a dousing of ice-cold water on a hot flame – I was shut down. The idea held merit, but it was everything in between that caused the cold reaction. I felt like I was on trial with a defense lawyer asking;

"Have you considered first aid and safety"? – response 'No'

"Have you thought about making shirts"? – response 'Not yet'

"Have you thought of a date"? – response 'no'

"What about advertisement"? – you should be able to guess what the answer would be.

When she asked me where my proposal was, I must have had the stupidest look on my face but I was so glad that I had asked my father to wait in the adjacent room, this way he wouldn't think his son was such a moron. I had no idea what a proposal was and not to mention I felt so deflated that I wanted to leave the room without saying good-bye, let alone a thank-you. I left the office humbled, and was glad when dad gathered by my body language and lack of excitement that it didn't go over so well, however, on the bright side at least she liked the idea!

It shall be stated for the record, that I am no expert in the things that I do – the phrase – 'Jack of all traits, but master of none' comes to mind to put it bluntly. I was a young optimistic teenager walking into the office that would serve me one of the most humbling experiences of my life but I walked out alive. In the months and years that followed, I learned that I am not afraid to fail and trust me, failure is as common as the amount of ice cream that I eat which, take my word for it, is quite a bit. Our world is littered with great speakers and motivators who claim that if it wasn't for their failure they wouldn't be where they are today. Many of the world's leaders in their autobiographies and memoires reflect on their moments of failure as the most character building experiences of their lives. I couldn't agree more – failure builds character – simple as that! However, unless you have put yourself in a position where the potential of failure has the power to revoke all your energy, your visions and your dreams, there is very little room for character building to take place. One of the things that I walk on egg shells for are other people's dreams. The reason is that they are powerful to that particular individual and they mean something more than I could imagine to that person and if I was insensitive or straight out rude, the potential to crush a spirit is devastating. Once the spirit goes so does the will.

Walking out of the President's office at Sick Kids hospital was devastating for me. I'm sure you'll agree that most of us have had dreams shattered or spirits damaged and rarely have gathered the strength to try once again on that dream or great idea. It happens all the time, some of us are so fearful of the thought of failure we cocoon ourselves against it. Needless to say, you look at failure in one of two ways, you succumb to it and conform, or you rise above and thrive. God helped me with the latter and I was able to recover from a point of not wanting to help people ever again, to doing things I never would have imagined if I was satisfied with trying once and accepting failure. Just like Andrew said when we started the trek down Yonge Street to raise awareness and money for Big Brothers and Big Sisters of York – 'it is the thought of fear and not fear itself that keeps us from trying'. With God's grace I have dived into more unknown territory than I can count and when I landed, committed, determined with the slightest clue on how to proceed, I'd say a prayer and asked for the vision and leadership necessary to take my vision from playful idea to real time success and it has worked every time. When it doesn't, I sit back and calculate that there was a reason and look for the learning experience that comes from a perceived fail which by default makes it a positive experience – if you're the type of person that sees the cup as half full.

The concert that we held for Greg on February 2nd at the University of Guelph had its proceeds donated to *Guelph Community Living* which advocates for, promotes, and facilitates the full participation, inclusion and empowerment of people who have an intellectual disability. With our efforts we were able to raise over $6,000 en masse for the organization and simultaneously make Greg's dream come true. However, the concert was much more than that, it was a gateway for a thought process that would encourage Andrew and me to consider opening up our own charitable organization. With much thought and prayer, we believed that if it was God's will then all we had to do was apply for charitable status and with that, the application was submitted. The name that we submitted to Canada Revenue Agency for consideration was – The Five with Drive Foundation. When the lines were dotted and the 'T's crossed, it was officially out of our hands, and in all honesty we were content to leave it in God's hands for the result.

In conjunction with the concert that we hosted that year, there was another plan that started to plant its roots in the hearts of Andrew and me. Those living with intellectual disabilities were not just a passion that dwelled inside of me; Andrew had also taken on a compassionate heart for those living under the label of 'disabled'.

As I was entering my final year at the University of Guelph, I caught myself on the main drag of the campus, which is known as 'Winegard'. I haven't the slightest idea as to the origin of the name, however, it served as a pedestrian highway that connected the north end of the campus to the south, in a red bricked, hand packed walkway. Thousands of students would traverse Winegard each day, to and fro they went and occasionally I would sit back and watch the traffic of human bodies. It was September and I noticed one student who I hadn't seen before walk with an over compensating limp on the bricks of Winegard. I noticed that his knees would bow inwards, and his upper-torso was thrown harshly in the opposite position as his legs swung to and fro. I later discovered that the student had a physical condition called cerebral palsy, a condition that affects the central nervous system that results in motor-skill difficulty or in extreme cases it will leave someone a quadriplegic. It is a condition that one is born with and let me clear the mind – it is not contagious!

As he was making his way to his next commitment, my focus was on him, it just seemed as though no one was stopping to say hi or walk with him, his pace was drastically slower than everyone else's and it seemed an inconvenience for those who were held up behind him waiting to pass. My thoughts travelled to the upcoming winter and I wondered how well he would manage when the ground became slick with ice. 'Surely this guy has fallen before in the winter' I said to myself. All these thoughts were transpiring so quickly that before I knew it I was in front of him, introducing myself. I'm sure he found it odd that some random fellow would come introduce himself amidst a frenzy of students just to say 'hello'.

That night I called Andrew and as smooth as I could have ever been, I asked, "Hey, what do you think about walking from Halifax, Nova Scotia, to Markham, Ontario – Andrew quickly responded with, 'and raise awareness and monies for people living with disabilities?" I was shocked, yet elated Andrew was in and had the same heart I had making it for people living with disabilities. By this point in our relationship Andrew has come to expect that every now and then I would call with crazy ideas so he doesn't bother being shocked anymore.

"Ya, Dan that sounds good, how about we talk about it later." Hardly the response I was looking for at the time. However, it didn't take Andrew long before he was full swing on board with the idea and soon after that we adopted the idea of walking from Halifax to Markham, a trek that would cover more ground than Yonge Street; amass over 2,500 kilometers, take 45 days and multiple shoes.

Our goal was to highlight the lives of people living with intellectual disabilities, and not allow society to discredit their abilities through stereotyping and ignorance. At this point, people in the Markham area had been introduced to and were familiar with the name we chose to walk Yonge Street under – Five with Drive. Building on that reputation was paramount on this walk. Part of the mission statement that we provided Canada Revenue Agency in our application package for charitable consideration was to raise awareness and funds for vulnerable groups of people in our society and educate the masses to reduce stigma and stereotyping associated to marginalized groups. In a biblical sense our mission statement reflects the words of 1 John 3:18 which were recited earlier.

Andrew was quick to choose a Markham organization that worked with adults living with disabilities past the age of 21. In Ontario, children with disabilities are integrated into public and/or catholic schooling up to the age of 21, in which they have to graduate and then, for a lack of a better term, are dumped. Very little post-secondary opportunities exist for adults with intellectual disabilities and after the age of 21 parents begin the tedious march to find social activities for their children to become involved with and more importantly continue to develop socially and independently. There are very few organizations that cater to adults with disabilities and the ones that do exist are under-funded, under-staffed and over worked!

Andrew and I recruited another three guys bringing our total to 5 and a bit symbolic of our previous fundraiser walk. On our team we had one original member of the Five with Drive team returning, Mark MacDonnell and two new members. One was Marcel Destine who was in Greg and the Boys and was on a road of recovery with different aspects of his life at the time and the intention of bringing him was to allow him to escape the temptations that he was facing and be surrounded with positive reinforcement and a trip of a life-time. The last member, who was our youngest, was Rob Skelly. Rob was in the Military with me and was a fireball of action and energy and I thought that mixed with Andrew and Marcel the three of them would bring the energy and excitement the trek needed and in Mark and I, the stability and responsibility to level it out.

Individually we were unique and brought different components to the challenge but collectively we were poised on altering the perception of those living with intellectual disabilities. Andrew and I reflected on the experience of Yonge Street and we consciously wanted to make this endeavor more integrated with platforms to share our message with. The walk was to start two weeks after I graduated, which meant that elementary and high schools were still in session on the east coast and that became a vested interest of ours to target young minds and equip them with the message we wanted to share. The other aspect that we kindled was meeting up with organizations that worked for adults with disabilities from Halifax to Markham. With our goals in sight, it would take nine months to turn our idea into reality.

Greg – would constantly remind us of how important it was that we were doing this walk for him, a statement that none of us would correct him on.

The task that we set ahead of ourselves was daunting at times, what was more straining was not the distance that we decided to cover, it was the 60 days of employment that the 5 of us would forego to pursue the cause we all believed in. It was clear from the beginning that no one was to receive a stipend or donation for participating in the walk, all monies were held for our overhead cost and for the organization we identified to receive the funds.

Andrew couldn't help but feel bad for the position that we were putting our father in, Dad has a small construction business and for years relied on Andrew and me as his work horses to manage and operate the business and with both of us gone for such a lengthy period, Dad was bound to have long days and stressful moments as he would have to find replacements. Andrew's way of bringing ease to the situation was to say, "You can't replace these guys", and then flex his biceps, making his point more illustrated. The fact was, that all five of the members who accepted the walk were giving up something that summer but in return gaining everything. I was amazed that four young men would freely give up employment and their summer to undertake the journey. Some men are focused on establishing their lives at that young age and many wouldn't have had the patience to take the time I was asking for to speak against the injustices of how people with disabilities were treated by society. I salute the members of Five with Drive, your courage and dedication is remarkable.

For a team building foundation, we left Markham for Halifax in our outfitted truck and trailer, decaled with our message and sponsor logos, a week and a half before we started our trek. It would take 2 days of driving, one overnight stay in the Sobey's parking lot in Woodstock, New Brunswick and $700.00 dollars in gas to make it to Halifax. Graciously, a friend through the Salvation Army had arranged a temporary shelter for us to lodge at before we started our walk. What he didn't tell us right away was that the place was a drop in house in the projects of Halifax in an area known as Uniacke Square.

The 'Square' as it was referred to had a horrible reputation and illustrated by Urban dictionary as:

"Uniacke Square: a crime-ridden gathering of apartment buildings built a block down from Gottingen Street in Halifax, Nova Scotia, Canada. 100% inhabited by black people.... No sane white person should ever walk down through Uniacke Square at night..." (UrbanDictionary.com)

What a horrible reputation, it couldn't have been that bad since right up the street from us was a community police station which still didn't provide much reassurance for my team – which had four white members and one black and Marcel would joke that he'd be fine but he didn't know about our safety!

God will never place you in a situation you can't handle, and this was not out of our league. Being the new kids on the street the first night was the worst. Our new donated Dodge truck was getting more attention than any other car on the street and the 5 of us started tossing a baseball in front of the house to block out the stares that were received from the local habitants. A member of the police force stopped by at the end of his shift and told us that a man was stabbed the night before and for us to be careful if we were staying in the 'Square'. When we told him that we were staying for a week, he nearly doubled over. Truthfully, I don't think any of us were overly fearful that this was that bad of a place.

The staff that ran the programming out of the house held their last session the next day for the children of the neighborhood – and were taking a week's holiday to take advantage of us staying in their place of work. The house was in the middle of a block of 30 homes all attached and the community was a series of block homes. The poverty was visible to the eye and the associated problems also very apparent. From our window at night we would watch drug deals, prostitutes flagging down 'Johns', and pimped out cars just cruising around as though they were conducting night patrol – their tinted windows were enough for me to think the worst of those inside – drug dealers or murderers – I couldn't decide.

For the days leading up to the walk our agenda was filled with school presentations, which we would average around two a day, soft-ball games with local high school groups, team workouts and something that we did not expect to happen in the slightest, unknown to us, the staff that ran the social centre that we were lodged at failed to inform the children of Uniacke Square that after school programs were suspended until they returned. Our second day in the square we had returned from speaking with high school students about our message and entered our temporary residence exhausted and seeking our sleeping bags. Just as our eyes had started to close, we heard banging on the front door. The noise startled us to our feet – the knocking was loud and had it been night-time, I'm sure none of us would have hesitated to call the police right away. The banging got louder we made our way down the stairs andas the lock was slid open, the door exploded inwards and a barrage of children ran into the house, up the landing and invaded the open space that served as the arts and crafts section of the house. It was a whirlwind of action and confusion and initially the five of us were trying to herd up the mass of obnoxious children.

When the exodus wasn't happening and the 15 or so kids who were cramped into the tiny open space began to raise the noise level beyond recognition, I yelled, "Woaaaaaaa! Slow down, what's going on here"?

One of the girls who was the natural leader of the group, who reminded me of a very small Queen Latifa, put her hand on her hip and with the faintest bit of attitude, said,

"We's always get our freeze pops here after school!"

"Alright, well if we give you a freeze pop will you guys leave?"

"Nopes, we's then draw or play outside",

This girl was driving a hard bargain so I agreed to the freeze pops, and Rob, Andrew and Marcel who have all worked in a camp capacity were quick to improvise and take care of the social activities. The next thing you know, tables were set up and blank pieces of paper were in front of the kids sitting on chairs around the table and drawing commenced. Under the supervision of Rob, Andrew and Marcel the kids were captivated with the older boys who were encouraging their random creative pieces.

When the ordeal was over, and the clean up complete, the time that had lapsed was two hours. The guys agreed to hosting the kids again the next day and in all honesty I don't know if we had an option. The next day as we released the kids from an after school scavenger hunt that we had set up, we noticed that the kids all ran to their respective homes and were in instant conversation with either their mother or father figure, with the occasional glance up from their guardians, we thought that everything was kosher! Just as we were thinking that everything was happy go lucky, 'Queen Latifa's mom and the little darling herself snuck up on us, wanting to know some answers.

"First" her voice was deep and hoarse, "ya'll cops or what"? Whew! A sigh of relief swept over us, 'No ma'am, were not cops", one of my friends assured her. "Than what'd ya'll doin here in the square? You da new staff taking over the after school drop in for the kids?" She was determined to find out who we were.

"Ma'am, we aren't cops, we aren't social workers, and we aren't taking over the drop in, we are here for a couple of days and then starting a walk home to

Markham, Ontario for a fundraiser to support people with disabilities."

"Ya'll doin, WHAT....yous crazy", and with that comment she scooped up her daughter and turned back into the direction that she came from, chuckling all the way back. When she reached her abode, she yelled back and said, "Well, yous better make sure that you show up for our yearly BBQ, the mayor's going to be there and the PO-lice be doing the cooking." Enough said, her words were like music to our ears and she definitely knew how to sweet-talk a bunch of young men by offering food!

Our time at Uniacke Square was like walking back in time to the early 1960's when racism against black people was rampant. During one of our school presentations at a high school within the vicinity of the square our usual message that we shared met a solid wall of racism. When we walked into the classroom of grade 12 students, there was a divide splitting the class like the 'Red Sea', on one side there were the black teenagers that lived in the area we were staying in and on the other side were the white kids. Even before we started our presentation I knew that we would be talking about something completely different than what we had planned. You could feel the tension between the two groups. When we engage kids in whatever venue, our set up was the same. I would stand in front of our audience and the four other guys would disperse themselves amongst the audience. This was deliberate, for one, it helped with crowd control and second it wasn't I that would start our engagement. A common distraction mechanism, everyone's attention would fall onto the front of the class awaiting the introduction and formalities when receiving a presentation. When the guys in the audience would stand up and introduce themselves, and then start on their choreographed opening. It worked well for our group and by the time the guys were finished, the audience would know exactly what we had set before ourselves and why we chose such a noteworthy event. By the time I would open my mouth, 10 minutes usually had passed. One of the benefits for me observing out was the ability to watch everyone in the audience – pick out those that were attentive – potential problem makers – and read how people were receiving our message.

This presentation was no different, the boys stood in the aisles that they each had claimed drawing the student's reaction immediately, I merely observed. The first thing that struck out in all our minds was the black and white divide. It seemed as though the Caucasian and whiter skinned teenagers were on one side of the divide and on the other sat the black students. Without them saying a word, I knew that there was a barrier between the two distinct groups. As the boys were introducing themselves, I knew that the students wouldn't be interested in our quest to help people with intellectual disabilities and decided to address the often-hostile topic of racism.

"Stalin, the communist ruler of the Soviet Union once said that the death of a million is a statistic and the death of ONE is a tragedy. Racism, if it doesn't kill you, has the power to kill your spirit and that can result in something I call the living dead – alive in the world – dead in spirit."

I have never been formally educated in public presentations but I do know that if you don't get an audience in your introduction you'll be struggling to gain their attention. There was this white kid, who kept speaking throughout each of our introductions – and after the opening line I called him out, "You're being rude – if you have something to say, by all means share with all of us". The kid had a hat sideways on his head, his clothing was three to four. "I think there's nothing wrong with niggers working for us". I couldn't believe what I had just heard and the room erupted into verbal chaos between the two groups and it took minutes to settle the crowd down again.

"White, Yellow, Black or Red – Chinese, African, Indian or American we all bleed the same colored blood". The black kids jumped into the conversation and went off on the fact that they were oppressed by white business

178

owners and white people in general who won't hire them because of their color and further treated them different. Even though this was happening right in front of us I found it so hard to believe that this form of racism was still happening.

There were no miracles that day – no moments of enlightenment from our perspective regarding the students we spoke with. I don't know how we did it but somehow we spoke for an hour or so with the students about social respect for all cultures and the social fabric of equality concerning all persons. To the surprise of the white kids in the class when we mentioned that we were temporarily living at Uniacke square their mouths dropped in utter shock. They couldn't fathom four white guys and one black guy living in the confines of Nova Scotia's most notorious criminal neighborhood – on the plus side that won us some respect among the black students.

There exists no metric system to calculate victory in stories such as this, however, that night when we returned to our humble abode in the square, some of the black students we had spoken with during the day had stopped by to say hello. To me, above all that is success – something during the hour talk we gave that day struck a note with the two students that stopped by, perhaps it was to verify that indeed we were staying in the square, or perhaps it was because they wanted to share their stories with us or like I said, something that was said hit home and their visit with us was their way of telling us that it made sense. Who knows?

Timing can be everything and I am of the belief that everything happens for a reason, nothing is by chance and that God is the mastermind of the collection of moments that we live on this earth – our time is definite and agreeably short, just a whisper in the wind – here one minute and gone the next. Understandably, I know this is not the belief that everyone shares and that this belief is particular to me, yet, because I view life in this way, it allows me to appreciate the moments, good or bad that God places me in.

A BARBEQUE AT UNIACKE SQUARE

By the end of our stay at Uniacke Square, Five with Drive were preparing for the BBQ that was being held the day prior to us taking our first step towards home.

Uniacke Square was jumping, the day was beautiful, kids were outside, women were cooking up a storm and the police were laid back and enjoying the atmosphere. To make us stand out, the five of us wore our uniforms, easily identifiable we mingled through the crowds of neighbors. At one point, Marcel came rushing to my side to inform me that some of the men in the neighborhood thought that we were cops living among them, watching their activity and that we were playing with their kids as a cover up! Marcel had a big sigh of relief; I thought it was funny that the suspicion we received from the men in the neighborhood was because we were regarded as police officers. I can't blame the men for thinking that either, the five of us were in great shape, held our confidence in body posture, clean-shaven and three out of the five were still in the Military at the time. Now that the secret was out that we weren't cops, the men that had mostly ignored our presence had opened up at least to say hi to us during the BBQ.

It wasn't long before the five of us were the life of the party. Once the music started, so did the conga-lines lead by Rob as we gathered all the kids in and some of their daring mothers and danced around the gathering. The police had no idea who we were and were surprised we were still alive, when we told them of our stay at the Square and that our donated Dodge Ram 1500 had not been broken into and stolen! The Chief of Police for Halifax thought that we were police officers from Ontario as he had received a phone call from York Region's, Chief of Police letting each province know of our coming and going and had requested escorts through all major cities from Halifax to Toronto.

Ironic as it may be, since the writing of this book, two of the five men that were a part of the Five with Drive team in 2007 are now active police officers. The Mayor of Halifax was present as well and showed no hesitation to join the conga line that was started. The entire afternoon was a blast – the local kids gravitated to Marcel, Rob and Andrew and you could see the three of them enthusiastically involved in all of the games that were set up for the kids. Mark and I just took it all in.

Just as the party was coming to a close, a taxi could be seen stopping at the bottom of the hill, and out popped, mom and dad! There was no expectation that they would come out to see us off and the surprise was pleasant, their timing was perfect because if it had been an hour later the BBQ's would have been shut down.

When the time came to close our adventure in Halifax, we couldn't have been more ready to start the 45-day trek home. We decided to start on a Sunday, and take our first steps off the summit of Capitol Hill in downtown Halifax. The morning we met had a slight enough chill to keep us in our warm hoodies as we stood on top of the hill taking in the view of the city and the seaports that boasts of Halifax's beauty and history. We were joined by many people on top of the hill that morning, the presence of NDP Alexa McDonough, Liberal MP Lui Temelkovski, Mayor of Halifax Peter Kelly, pastors, a few students, mom and dad and the media were all present as we formed our circle and linked arms. The circle was large by the time the last arms were linked and the task ahead even longer. Without a doubt, I wanted all to know that our inspiration wasn't the adventure of the walk, nor the moments of fame we received during our presentations or meeting numerous dignitaries, nor was it the beauty of doing something unique and different – our inspiration was the people we set out to help with every step we took – those living with intellectual disabilities – when all was said and done and a prayer over our protection ended with an, Amen, Five with Drive's journey of a thousand steps began.

Our routine was similar to when we walked Yonge Street – Reveille was at 0330 hrs in the morning, and four of the five team members would start their day of 50 kilometers. We had a rotation that every day, one of the team members would drive our truck and trailer and it would be their responsibility for meals, clean up and following the group. We quickly came to know who the good cooks were compared to the not so good cooks. Walking 50 km's a day is strenuous on the body and usually took 9-11 hours to complete the pre-determined mileage. When we had school presentations, the kilometers subsided, but usually resulted in an added 10 or 15 kilometers for the day after presentations.

Our last set of school presentations were held in New Brunswick, prior to the summer break that was pending. We stayed a total of three days in New Brunswick at a hotel that lent their lodging to us. We would drive to the previous day's end point, and start the new day from there, walk straight through to lunch and then head back for a school presentation in the afternoon.

New Brunswick was great for their support and the schools would gather in their gyms filled with students to hear the message we were sharing. On our last day of presentations, as we re-entered the city limits, an accident in front resulted in emergency personnel closing down the road temporarily. Fearful at first that we might miss our opportunity to speak at our last engagement, Andrew, Rob, Marcel and I took off running through the streets to the school that we were expected at. Mark arrived when the road re-opened.

After walking, at that point, for twenty days, running felt unexplainably awkward. Our legs burned with built up lactic acid as they pumped towards the school. At our arrival we were knackered, sweaty and in desperate need of a drink. We were greeted at the door by the principal who commented on our impeccable timing. "The students are all in the gym, awaiting your introductions" he said, as he led us towards the gym. Where was the glass of water that we wanted more than anything?

He certainly was right; the gym was packed from the second floor rows that sat the older students to the pull out bleachers on the main floor and the hundreds of students sitting on the floor. As the team took their seats among the masses, I was led to the stage. There was a microphone and a screen behind it that would play our video for the students. As the team was making their introductions, my legs started to shake with fatigue as I stood in front of the gathering and the shaking became so bad that I couldn't concentrate on my words and finally succumbed to the fatigue and asked for a chair. My concentration returned when I took a seat and I stayed seated for the remainder of the presentation. For me, the best part of our speaking engagements was meeting the students with disabilities, usually before we took to the stage or immediately afterwards. It wasn't unusual for some of the younger kids to ask for autographs, why they would was beyond me, I felt like saying, "guys, honestly, we are nobodies, just regular guys and our autographs won't mean much at all!" Regardless of how I felt, I was glad that I was rarely in a position to sign autographs, rather I was watching the rest of my team give theirs freely which kept me from ruining the moment.

With all our attention we would listen to the children with disabilities share their excitement of meeting Five with Drive and what they were looking forward to during their day. Those moments were precious and I wouldn't trade them for anything in the world – it was our collective goal to make the students with intellectual disabilities feel as special as we could when we arrived in their school and we made a strong effort to try and learn their names.

When we started our walk, it upset me that Greg was graduating high school the same year and that I wouldn't be able to see him on a day that meant so much to him. The trade off was that the walk symbolized our passion we had for Greg and all those living with intellectual disabilities.

Despite not being able to attend Greg's graduation, Jenny and Harold – Greg's parents, brought Greg to Ottawa when we were passing through to spend a couple of days with us. In their generosity they also paid for a hotel for the team to stay at and enjoy a little civilization. Greg wanted nothing more than to spend every moment he had with us. Jenny and Harold didn't mind Greg's participation in our day as long as he didn't bother us. Although Greg didn't live in the sleeping quarters of our trailer, he pretty much did everything else. Greg would walk a couple of kilometers with us in the morning, and then be totally satisfied spending the rest of the day in the support vehicle. We usually had a break every 5 kilometers, and when Greg was on board he made our breaks memorable. At times you could hear Greg cheering us on 500 meters away as we approached the folding chairs that he helped set up with the drinks he had helped place in the cup holders. Greg would always turn the music up in the truck when we arrived and graciously give up his seat to one of us and go around patting everyone's shoulders. Greg has this teddy bear hug that he gives when he sees me without fail and even though I would be sweaty he would still give me a hug when I approached. Greg was so proud of us! That is how success is measured – metric conversion does not exist to quantify success – a spirit touched is more prosperous than any dollar amount.

The other thing about Greg is that he has one of the healthiest appetites I've ever come across and when saying that, he will keep eating until you have to tell him to stop or literally take his food away. The five walkers were justified in eating a copious amount of food and to fit in Greg would join in our feasting. His excuse was that we were working hard and he was here to support us!

I took an afternoon off from walking to drive the support vehicle and spend time with Greg. Greg and I can talk about some immature stuff at times and listen to music so loud that it would make a grandfather turn in his grave. That afternoon I drove with Greg and it was nothing but laughter and fun. We must have had two ice-caps putting him close to being over his allotted limit set by his parents of three a week! But, I think special times call for special allowances and this certainly granted one! If we could, we would choose our break location in a Tim Horton's parking lot, it was Greg's idea and if we were tossing a baseball or Frisbee, we were always catching up on good times. Greg has this remarkable memory, in which, he remembers the funny moments that our friendship has created and re-lives them with the same spell of laughter each time. I expressed to Greg and his parents that the team wanted him to walk the last 10 kilometers of our walk with us when we approached Markham, as a matter of fact, it would be an honor if Greg would join us! When I told Greg, his response was quick and impactful, "Daniel....I love you", and usually when he uses those words it's followed with one of his teddy bear hugs!

THE LAST STRETCH

It took us a week of tireless days walking from Ottawa before we reached the outer border of York Region and the last 10 Kilometers of the walk. As requested, Greg was ready and waiting to finish the walk with us and to help him look like one of the Five we gave him a team uniform that helped him fit in better. The descent towards the fin-ish line took us down Highway 7 in Markham enroute with the municipal government buildings that encased the fin-ish line. From a distance we could hear noise erupting from the crowd that had gathered by the end mark, at the time it was extremely hard to believe that the jour-ney was coming to an end, that the 45 days it took from Halifax to Markham was about to finish its course. When we emerged on the last 100 meters of the walk, the now six of us with Greg in the middle all linked arms for the final steps – behind us we were joined by adults living with vary-ing disabilities heading for the finish line. Emotion overtook us all in different ways and all we could manage was a smile. The crowd that had gathered was larger than we had expected and the music that was playing filled the atmosphere with a champion's ending. Friends, family and local officials had gathered to welcome our comple-tion and to congratulate our efforts.

Throughout the walk we had to constantly re-direct the praise we would receive towards the people that we were serving, for those that inspired our call to action. At the closing ceremonies there were numerous reflections on 'our' efforts, there was talk about the distance we covered, the difficult passages and the determination 'we' had. I suppose that you have to include these types of sentiment to give the audience an understanding of what has taken place. Personally, I found that it was easy for others to focus on what they might call the 'sacrifice' that these five men have made. That never sat right with me, in my mind there is only one person that has sacrificed, and that is Jesus Christ, when he died on the cross for our sins. The five of us that undertook this walk would not describe our act as a sacrifice, rather a more modest approach of 'sharing' out time to help others. To us sacrifice evokes a form of heroism in the giving up of something to achieve something else. The word is powerful and 'sacrifice' in my eyes can only be redeemed for those that truly 'sacrifice' their life for another. In our case, we took 60 days out the 365 days a year and the thousands of days that we had lived on the earth until we had crossed the finish line to support others that are marginalized in society. We took our time to 'share' with others and highlight the lives of disabilities – there was never a sacrifice.

The message conceived to the crowd that day was no different than what has just been shared except this time, emotion overtook my senses and as I looked through the faces of the people that had gathered and saw the joy and tears of support in their expressions, tears began to well in my eyes and drop freely onto the podium that I stood behind.

When the party had settled down and people started to leave, the five of us marched straight up to an ice cream truck that was on scene and enjoyed a much-anticipated ice cream! We must have made that ice-cream look so good because it appeared on the first rendition of 'Snap' Markham, a newspaper that captures all the excitement in Markham through pictures.

CHAPTER FIFTEEN

BACK IN CONCERT MODE

Keep on singing and dancing –
it makes the world go round!

- Unknown Artist

Greg and the Boys went into full forward throttle after the walk. Marcel had moved on and was no longer an active member of the band and his spot was quickly filled with the enthusiastic and dedicated Rob Skelly. It was a natural progression for Rob – I had invited him to our first concert in Guelph, Ontario and he was the first person in the audience that I saw singing along with us to the Backstreet Boys.

During the walk, Rob would graciously entertain us with his selection of music that ranged from famous boy bands to Avril Lavigne. Rob brought to the band, a fresh set of ideas and enthusiasm with organizing concerts.

Greg was in his element with the band back together and regular practices starting up again and it didn't take long for Greg to begin sharing his dreams of performing with us. However, this time around they were a little different; "Dan, how cool would it be to sing in Hollywood." It's hard to say no to Greg at times "Well...I think that would be pretty cool but I don't think that we are ready for Hollywood or that Hollywood is ready for us". Greg would just respond with an exaggerated 'Come onnnnnnn'.

Greg's next biggest thought at the time was performing with Carrie Underwood, the country pop star and one time American Idol and that was definitely out of our league and I'm sure the stars would have to align just right for Miss Underwood to even take knowledge of us let alone consider a performance with us but that's what dreams are for! I would tell Greg to hold on to that one and wrote it down in my memory bank for when Carrie Underwood came to Toronto for her next performance and try to get tickets.

Talk of another concert in Markham began to take fruition and before we knew it the members of Greg and the Boys were in full swing organizing a concert at the Markham Theatre that could sit 525 people.

Still passionate about helping those with disabilities, we conceived an idea that we dubbed as an educational concert that would have entertainment and keynote presentations that would engage the audience with an introduction to what a life with disabilities entails.

We had chosen another small organization in the Markham area that worked directly with people living with intellectual disabilities to receive a portion of the funds we raised and access to the exposure that we were hoping to create. In their agreement they had also accepted the invitation to put on a presentation of their own during the concert with their members – an act that would assist with illustrating the purpose of our event.

Greg was in cruise control – practicing, ice-caps and hanging out with his boys brought all the happiness to his life. By far, this concert would surpass any of our previous performances in regards to audience attendance and singing in a theater that is well known as a reputable stage for professional performers.

Our practices were usually held one night a week and we would joke that we could only take one night a week of Backstreet Boys because we were afraid of losing our choice of music to the pop culture. A few weeks before the concert, the band took a trip to the Markham Theatre to walk around before the show! When empty, the theater looks enormous and majestic, the cascading seating arrangement leads to a flat black raised stage with full curtains, spot lights and all the prospects of a night full of excitement. Greg was speechless when he entered the theater, his fear of heights took over him and step by tedious step one of the boys led him down the stairs towards the stage. Greg kept telling us how he thought that this was so cool and that he couldn't wait until the performance!

Back stage was just as impressive – change rooms with full mirrors and individual bathrooms, a green room and a full kitchen gave the feel of the real deal for our amateur group. The concert couldn't come any sooner!

The months leading up to our Markham Theater performance were filled with smaller performances mostly at permanent facilities for people with disabilities in York Region and

Guelph. We also took a trip down to McMaster University where we performed for their medical facility. Greg's confidence was growing with each performance and the change in his comfort level was drastic. By this point, Greg no longer had lyrics in his face and was singing more and more like he would in practice. Greg would still wear his sunglasses but would momentarily take them off during parts of a song when he wanted to get the crowd going. Greg would deflect questions that people had for him towards one of the boys and when I would share the story of how Greg and the boys came about, he would jump in every now and then if I got the sequence of events mixed up!

Greg was finding his way in life. Unfortunately, most people with disabilities have the same social groups that mostly consist of people with similar life circumstances and the compassionate social aid workers that spend their time with them. It is very rarely that someone with a disability finds themselves in a group outside of their norm and on top of that, accepted by an outside group. Greg had the benefit of both worlds – he was a role model for his friends who looked up to him and always inquired about 'his' band, in which he was never short of updating them on. Greg would constantly be asked from his friends if they could try out for the band. When they would ask him, it was a straight phone call to me asking for my advice. In all truthfulness, we held a couple of try-outs for some of Greg's friends but found that it wasn't the same and each friend had a different element that they brought, a talent that just didn't fit, but a talent nonetheless. At the end, we would always agree that 'Greg and Boys' was a story on its own and that's how we would keep it. When we would perform at school functions, we would include our biggest fans, the kids with exceptionalities somehow in our performance – whether we share our mics during the choruses of a song or get right in the middle of a group of dancers and sing with them, we would always reward the support we received from these kids which also made them feel very much a part of the band and the questions to join the band that Greg received would subside.

Greg and the Boys were invited back to an interview with Rogers Television, the oh so familiar territory of a studio with the treatment that went along with it, to make you feel like a true star. This time around the Boys weren't play fighting in the green room but the stage co-coordinator hadn't forgotten the ruckus that they had caused the first time around and reminded us that she expected our best behavior.

The weekend before our concert, Greg's former teaching assistant Mai Lin Bozian, from his late high school, hosted us at her cottage to put our act together and relax before the show. It was never a dull moment; Mai's cottage is magnificent, the serenity is stunning and the best part was that the food would just keep coming. Our stage was the back deck that overlooked the lake, which made an impressive view that served as our audience.

When the concert had arrived, we were busy shuttling all the necessary items to the theater hours before our dress rehearsal. The spirit that was between Greg and the Boys was contagious. We showed up in the parking lot to unload posters and props – rocking to 'Miley Cyrus'! The five of us were piled into Rob's truck, music blaring and when we stopped at the loading bay, we each got out and danced the remaining two minutes of the song. After the song, a deep sense of exhaustion took over, if you have ever danced so hard and with so much passion put into every move, every twist and turn with nothing to fear, without caring who's watching and what they are thinking, when you just let loose it's exhausting. Just as the song finished, the back doors opened and our interior decorators were staring with confusion as we each struggled to catch our breath. Our energy rolled into the theater and the party kept going. The other group of disabled performers was completing their dress rehearsal run and Greg and the Boys took up front row seats to cheer them on. We did everything we could to make them feel like stars that day, with constant encouragement on and off the stage.

The best part of the concert for me was the opportunity to hang out with Greg, embrace the entirety of the event, share in the moments of laughter and not have to worry about people not doing their jobs to make this a success or not. This was big for us, big for Greg and it felt so good to be a part of Greg's Dream in a very intimate way. The most satisfying element of it all was that it didn't cost us a thing except for the TIME, life's most valuable commodity, the piece of life that we seek to prolong and acquire more of and all we had to do was offer and invest our time with Greg.

Prior to the show a college student studying journalism and film received our permission to conduct interviews with Greg and the Boys for a brief documentary that she would submit for marking at her school. The invitation brought a sense of stardom for Greg, while the rest of us tried to act as though the camera was not around. We all watched as Greg was interviewed in our change room. He was nervous, I liken he was more nervous being asked questions from a beautiful girl than sitting in front of a rolling camera. Greg's truthful, innocent answers brought a smile to our faces, the kind of smiles that make your cheeks sore. The last segment of filming was the linking of arms by all performers as we formed our circle in the green room. The show was about to begin.

LARGER THAN LIFE

The opening to our act was dynamic, darkness fell over the theater, the brilliant sounds of thunder rolling through the sound systems, artificial lighting orchestrated the flashes of lighting, temporarily illuminated the faces of those in the audience. Faintly in the background, 'Larger than Life' by the Backstreet Boys started to play, as the music escalated Andrew hit his opening line as a spot light followed him down the aisle towards the stage. Right after Andrew's part, Rob began his descent towards the stage, still darkened, still motionless. Miles, Greg and I were eagerly waiting backstage for our queue that would bring us out and bring the stage to life. Without missing a beat Miles and I entered the stage as the lights, perfectly timed, lit up the stage as the four of us sang the chorus of *Larger Than Life*.

It's amazing how the mind multi-tasks during a performance. I will quickly admit that multi-tasking is a skill that I am continually developing and one that I'm not too gracious at. However, on stage, in front of hundreds of people, I have found my mind wandering to places far away from the stage. Greg missed his queue, which was to come out with Miles and me and as I was singing I thought that perhaps Greg was too nervous. By far, this was the largest crowd we had performed in front of to date. I thought that perhaps we were pushing Greg too hard, despite the fact that it was Greg's dream to be in a band and sing, it could have been us that became consumed with putting on the best show we could and in doing so may have overlooked Greg's feelings. There is much work that goes into planning a concert and during the process we tried very hard to include Greg in all aspects of the ordeal. We want to hear Greg's thoughts and his ideas, we talk about things that are way beyond Greg's years, overhead costs, ticket sales, volunteer scheduling and all the other details that fall into effect with such events. Greg will often sit through a meeting, quiet, listening, still, acting as though he knows what's going on but his head is down, reading the lyrics to the songs that we have chosen and only pops his head up to ask when we are going to practice!

When Greg didn't come out, emotion came over me, I thought of nothing else than being his friend and moving back stage to be with him, the only thing holding me back was the fact that the band decided that if Greg didn't come out and decided to sing back stage away from the spot light, the show would go on.

The best part of *Larger than Life* is the chorus;

> *"All you people can't you see, can't you see*
> *How your love's affecting our reality*

Every time we're down
You can make it right
And that makes you larger than life"

Our choreographed dance moves during the chorus is the only time that we have a synchronized movement on stage and get most of the crowd's response when we start to flex during the last part of the chorus to illustrate that we are larger than life. As the chorus was approaching, Greg came running through the curtain and took his rightful place at the center of our group. The crowd didn't let him down with their applause and cheers, it was so loud that none of the boys could hear themselves singing and I actually stopped and couldn't hold back my smile that stretched from ear to ear while my friend joined us on stage, confident to make his own entrance and singing his part!

Our performance at the Markham Theatre was our best effort to date for Greg and the Boys. The applause at the end of our show was more than any of us had expected. Greg was handed a bouquet of flowers from a friend of mine, which to this day, he still reminds us about. It's a euphoric feeling, one that is difficult to describe – you're tired, your mouth is dry, your cheeks are sore, well at least for me they are, and although you're spent and the adrenaline has since subsided and your heart rate settling, you want more, you want to start it all over again. I suppose that's what the big recording artists feel to some extent as well.

Life after any of our concerts returns quickly to normal. Greg usually soars on the flight path of the concert for weeks and for the rest of us, Rob, Andrew, Miles and myself, life resumes, we go back to work, the band life settle's down, practices tend to die down, but the one thing that continues is the friendship. The moments that bring us to stardom are short lived and the real glory for us happens when the curtains close, back stage is cleaned up and the money we raised has been donated. It was our friendship that brought us all together, that is what calls us back and that is where each of us finds the answer to our lives.

Up until our performance at the Markham Theatre I was the one that would pick Greg up from his house each time we would hang out. I would be the one Greg would call to share his life's excitement with, his stress, his laughter, his stories. I looked at this part of our friendship as a testimony of how close we had grown over the years. Now, the boys were stepping up at being Greg's friend, not that they weren't already but they didn't own their friendship with Greg really until after the concert. Greg was calling the boys on his own fruition and the boys would call him. Before I knew it, I was sharing 'my Greg time' with the boys. Greg would organize coffee outings and movie viewings independently with any one of the boys. Although this is what I wanted, I couldn't help but feel a bit left out. Greg deserved to have real friends and be able to call them when he wanted. I was so used to being the one always at Greg's call, the sole friend in his life who he would call for everything and the one that, no matter what, had to take him to get his ice cap from Tim Horton's. I was proud that the boys had accepted Greg as their friend, truly accepted him. I was happy when outings were had and enjoyed without my being there. It was even a relief at times when one of the boys would pick Greg up and take him to our next group outing. It was all good, yet, I couldn't help but feel a bit jealous, not jealous in a bad way, but, in a way that allowed me to accept the fact that Greg had friends in return and was growing as a person because of it.

After the Markham Theatre performance, Greg and the Boys went on to host many smaller performances. We would travel wherever we were offered a spot to share our story. We went to McMaster University to sing and speak with the medical college, sang in front of 100 or so adults with intellectual disabilities at Participation House in Markham, we made the journey to Guelph to entertain *Guelph Community Living*, an organization that is doing tremendous work for adults with disabilities. No matter where we went, we went in style. Usually the final touches of our shows were put together during the car ride to the next performance – music blaring, men singing, it was a sight to see. I'd be the one that drove all the time and would just smile as the boys turned a simple car ride into a show not to miss.

Whenever we arrived at our final destination I learned over the years to keep a careful eye on the boys. They had burnt me once in the five years that we have been performing and that time came in our second year together, when we were asked to perform at a Christmas gathering held at a prestige golf course in the Markham area. It was one of our earlier shows and when we arrived at the golf course we were led to our change-room. Looking back we should have changed in the washroom, however, we were led to the club house change room which was nicer than anything that we had seen up until then. The place was extravagant, full size mirrors, lounge chairs, private showers and on the sink counters they had aftershave, cologne, shaving cream and hair gel. We only had a ten minute time delay before we were scheduled to perform and I told the boys that I would head up and present our song list and get things going on the technical side and that they were not to be any longer than a couple of minutes behind me! WELL, that was a mistake, the Master of Ceremonies for the event started to introduce Greg and the Boys...while Greg and the Boys were still in the change-room making themselves beautiful. I went on stage knowing full well what trouble the boys were causing and began telling the story of how we came to be. I was struggling towards the end of the story with words to say to keep the audience entertained when out of the corner of my eye a door opened and out stepped the boys. As they made their way to the stage I gave them a stare down of love and "you're all going to get it", as I got a strong whiff of the cologne and after shave that they had abused. At least they smelled pleasant. So, after that, no matter where we went to perform, they were constantly within observation from me.

CHAPTER SIXTEEN

AT THE END

'Daniel, YOU friggin kill me'!

- Greg O'Brien

It's amazing, at the writing of this book, I am in Calgary – 3,500 kilometers away from Greg and the Boys and feel a stronger tie for my friends than ever before. Perhaps, the old saying that 'distance makes the heart grow fonder' has some truth to it.

Greg is consistent with his phone calls and they truly make up the best part of my days. I try to answer all his calls just so he feels like I am there for him whenever he needs me to be. Although, the boy can call anywhere up to three to four times a day and my percentage for received calls lays somewhere around the 80% mark. I wish that I was just around the corner from Greg to pick him up, go for an ice cap and let conversation take us over. I believe that everything happens for a reason and because of that I know that God has brought me to where I am in the Canadian West for a reason and at times my lack of patience makes me feel like a little ship trying to navigate the vast blue ocean.

The story of Greg and the Boys continues – what started out as one boy's dream turned reality has evolved into a beautifully intricate series of friendships that has changed the lives of all those involved. I have encountered many people that are 'up front' nice and pleasant to people with intellectual disabilities and have seldom come across people that through their passion embrace everything that vulnerability has to offer and befriend a disability. Not to be construed as a cynic, there are plenty of compassionate souls out there that graciously lend their love and time to others with disabilities. The seldom part that I am referring to are the friendships that are created with complete strangers, like the one that Greg has with each of the boys.

In my absence I get to hear all the stories of what Rob, Andrew and Miles do to make Greg laugh on a weekly basis. I get to hear the frustrations from all of being in a band and more importantly I get to hear how Rob, Andrew and Miles are impacting Greg's life!

A couple of months before I left for the West, I took Greg to Ottawa to watch his favorite NHL hockey team play – The Ottawa Senators. On the trip up Greg listened to only one song, *Didn't Even See The Dust*, by Paul Brandt. It's a 4 hour drive from Toronto to Ottawa and trust me, Greg had no problem listening to that song over and over again. Every time he would replay it, he sang just as passionately as the first time he put it on. By the time we arrived in Ottawa, Greg and I knew that song inside and out! As a matter of fact, we knew it so well; the boys let us sing it as a duet for a concert that year.

Watching the Senators play was big for Greg and a dear friend of mine, Michele and her family, helped orchestrate the outing to allow Greg to experience his favorite team. Michele did such a fantastic job that she got two seats at ice level, behind the Senators goalie! We worked it out that every period, Greg would have someone different sitting with him. Michelle took the first period, her sister the second and I took the third. When we weren't sitting with Greg we took our seats up at the nose bleed section. I have never seen Greg so excited to watch hockey before in my life and when intermission came I could hear Greg yelling from his lower level seats from where I was. When time came for me to sit with my friend, the Senators were making their comeback from a two goal deficient and scored the equalizer and the go-ahead goal during our period, when each goal was scored, Greg cried. I joshed him a bit by saying, 'Greg, how can you be crying, your team just scored'? His sobs held him from answering and I was content with knowing that it was just the way Greg chose to experience the moment.

That night, when we lay our heads down, I on the floor and Greg on the bed, he asked me how to kiss girls!!! I laughed at first, and then told him that when he was 25 I'd tell him all the secrets!!!

On the way back from Ottawa – believe it or not, Greg listened to the same song the whole way back...well...partially, because when he fell asleep, I turned it off. My hesitation deciding whether to leave for a new experience in the West was filled with such thoughts of the moments that I would be missing and the friendships that I truly endear.

To complement our Ottawa trip, I was able to secure two seats to watch Carrie Underwood live at the Air Canada Centre and it just so happened that she was Greg's favorite singer! Greg was in his element, and sang every song from his seat 10 rows out. The only thing that we didn't see eye to eye on is whether Carrie blew a kiss to him or me – I still say me, since I'm taller and she probably couldn't see his much shorter self!

Although the struggle continues to exist with the distance between our friendships, I pray that it won't be forever and know that in my absence it is giving the boys the opportunity to get to know Greg on the level that he has blessed me with over the past twelve years.

ıGreg has taught me the concept of vulnerability as a kind of power. It's not always easy to see power in vulnerability in the painful mess of our world. Dad taught me to look for the presence of Jesus in the poor, the broken humanity within and around me and now I'll extend that perspective to those with disabilities, I can recognize Him in this indomitable drive to create, this joyous compulsion to liberate, and a tender, courageous vulnerability.ı

VULNERABILITY AND LOVE

Above all else the friendship that Greg and I enjoy has taught me what love and friendship truly mean. I turn to one of my favorite passages from the Bible to explain how Greg has impacted my life and how I truly believe that for the past 12 years I have entertained an angel.

If I speak in the tongues of men and of angels, but have not love, I am only a resounding gong or a clanging cymbal. If I have the gift of prophecy and can fathom all mysteries and all knowledge and if I have a faith that can move mountains, but have not love, I am nothing. If I give all I possess to the poor and surrender my body to the flames, but have not love I gain nothing.

Love is patient, love is kind, it does not envy, it does not boast, it is not proud. It is not rude, it is not self-seeking, it is not easily angered, it keeps no record of wrongs. Love does not delight in evil but rejoices with the truth. It always protects, always trusts, always hopes, always perseveres.

(1 Corinthians 13 1:10)

Life is a journey of unpredictable consequence, a struggle for identity and survival, a constant battling to survive and a desire to experience the best this world has to offer. When I look back to that day when I met Greg in the pool 12 years ago, I'm grateful for the courage that stirred inside of me to say 'hello'. Undoubtedly my life would have been different if I hadn't and I could not imagine a life without Greg.

There are thousands of people living with disabilities in our world, thousands suffer from the injustices of discrimination and isolation placed on them by society and thousands are waiting for YOU to say hello. A simple HELLO can make a world of difference.

Although this is the end of this book, it is not the end of Greg's and my friendship. Despite the distance, we still make *Greg and the Boys* work, it just costs me more to fly back to join the boys but the moments I spend with them are comparable to a thousand setting suns. Greg does an excellent job of keeping me updated with his life and all the little details that fill his days. I try to have a 'no drop call' quota with Greg, meaning that I try to answer every time he calls!

Until next time, May God Bless you, may He make you uncomfortable with injustices against the poor and destitute, May God give you the strength to use your voice to speak up against those injustices, May He make you unsatisfied with the status quo and give you energy to seek the truth. May God give you the courage to stand up for what is right and honest and keep your words pure and humble. May God make you discontent with material accumulation and give you the everlasting peace you get when you help another. May your days be filled with enthusiasm, good will and kind words.

AFTERWORD

I asked Greg to help pick the photo's that are present on each of the chapters. When Greg found out that I had written a book about our friendship I was bombarded with mass phone calls – thank God I have Greg on my FAB 10 plan because long distance charges would have gone through the roof!!!!

On April 1st, 2010 – Greg and the Boys performed a star studded show at Richmond Hill Theatre and release our newest material of songs from Frankie Valli and the Four Seasons raising awareness for the school in Kenya that the Five with Drive Foundation is working with, along with the revenue from ticket sales. Greg and the Boys have also been asked to perform for the first ever Canadian Special Olympics that will be held in Calgary in June, 2011 and I'm sure we'll keep singing as long as people continue to stay interested!

I personally want to thank you for taking the time to read this story. As I said before it is long from over and in many ways just starting and I look forward to how Greg and my friendship will grow as we are now both men! I look forward to the ice caps that I know we will share in the future and as promised when Greg turns 25 I will share all of my secrets about girls☺.

The proceeds from this book are going toward The Five with Drive Foundation and the work that we have set before us. I would love to share all the projects that we are involved with but would end up writing another book!!! Please visit our website at www.5wd.ca to see what we are doing in our community and around the world.

It was a pleasure for me to write this book and I hope that it was equally pleasurable for YOU to share in the story!

Made in the USA
Charleston, SC
06 April 2011